GRANDPA'S LESSONS ABOUT JESUS

EDWARD E. BROCK, JR.

Vigorous English 2014

GRANDPA'S LESSONS ABOUT JESUS
Published by Vigorous English
Noblesville, IN 46062 U.S.A.

ISBN-10: 0996006524
ISBN-13: 978-0-9960065-2-1
eBook ISBN: 978-0-9960065-3-8

Scripture quotations are from the King James Bible.

Cover Designed by Michael C. Duell

FOREWARD

Grandpa's Lessons About Jesus is a great read, but it's so much more than a beloved "coffee table book." It's a book that can trace its origins back to a 19th century circuit rider preacher arriving in a land populated by "seven-foot" tall giants, causing one to stop to see if they had accidentally picked a fantasy tale by J.R.R. Tolkien. It's a book born out of an idyllic Christian community in rural Indiana during the Great Depression that endured and spiritually thrived through their faith in God and loving, selfless compassion for one another; which unquestionably left an indelible impression on a young Edward Everett Brock, Jr. during his most formative years. It's a book packed with wisdom gained from his elders, the experience of World War II, time spent abroad, 40 plus years of work on the railroad, tragic personal loss, and an unquenchable thirst to seek, know, obey, and love Jesus. It's a book that despite its original intended audience, his seven grandchildren, has managed to find its way into the hands of hundreds of people desperately yearning to learn from Grandpa's lessons about Jesus.

While I would imagine Grandpa laments that the "Seven-Foot Community" he knew in his youth no longer exists, I cannot help but observe that he has in fact gone on to create comparable communities throughout his life and ministry inspired by that God inspired glimpse of the Holy City in "Seven-Foot." Unquestionably, this book is a direct influence of that time, and is also a historic document preserving the memory that such a place once existed, and the hope that it can exist again someday in the future.

Let me caution that in spite of the sentimental feeling the title may evoke, it's really a life changing book for any true seeker.

Please also note that although it's heavily influenced by his past experiences, it speaks clearly and directly to our future, where we will *all* either be eternally happy or eternally miserable. There is no middle ground.

It's a collection of sermons written and taught by a country pastor over the years, and yet Grandpa would ultimately tell you that he's only ever had one sermon over the years: the Cross. Bottom line, it's all about Jesus. He is not taking on social issues, debating doctrine, bemoaning modern worship, criticizing TV preachers, indoctrinating people about the age of the Earth, letting you know why God likes one political party better than another, or boasting of his own accomplishments. He simply teaches and preaches about Jesus, and how much He loves you, and wants to have an everlasting relationship with you. These are the lessons my Grandpa, my hero, taught me about Jesus. I sincerely pray that these thoughtful lessons impact you as they did me, and I am hopeful that the spirit of "Seven-Foot" will live on through your personal testimony.

Michael C. Duell
Grandson #2
Author of *The Rocky Raccoon Revival*
Noblesville, Indiana
2014

ACKNOWLEDGEMENTS

In memory of all of those dear people who attended The Otterbein United Brethren Church back when we were known as "Seven Foot."

Let the record show: In the beginning, there was a day in the year of 1881 when a circuit rider preacher, first held Church Services once a month in a little one room school house, which at the time was located across the road from our present church, Otterbein Church, located at 8243 South, County Road 900 East, Galveston, Indiana.

The name of the school was known as "7-Foot" because it was said, "Attending at this school were some extra tall boys." Well, maybe not 7-foot, but far taller than the average boy at that time. People would say, "There is where those 7-foot boys attend school." Hence the reason for the nickname "7-Foot."

When our church came into being, it adopted the name of "7-Foot" also. It became equally known as Otterbein or "7-Foot."

In the meantime the community around this "7-Foot" church for a mile or so in each direction, became known as "The 7-Foot Community."

The "7-Foot" community was different than most communities. The older generation was everybody's Grandpa and Grandma. The next generation was our Aunts and Uncles. We all claimed each other as cousins, even though we were not blood relatives. You might say, we were all just family, "The Family of God." Everyone for miles around knew where the "7-Foot" community was located.

It seemed as though we were always in one accord, in one accord with God.

From the beginning the words "7-Foot" was not just a physical and mental relationship, but it was a spiritual relationship.

It was a way of life. I repeat, "it was a way of life." It was love and compassion. It was a way of caring not only for ourselves, but also for all those we encountered.

It was not someone's imagination, not something I read in a book. It was not something I dreamed, but it was real. It was something I saw as a child, as a teenager, and as an adult. It was something I grew up with. It was something special. It seems as though God reached down and offered something special to a small community called "7-Foot," and they accepted it, and He blessed them.

In Revelation 21:3, God is telling John about a Holy City, the New Jerusalem coming down out of Heaven from God. He said, "The tabernacle of God is with men and He will dwell with them and they shall be His people and God Himself shall be with them, and He will be their God."

Years ago I think God reached down to a little community called "7-Foot" and said, "My children, here is a sample of the Holy City."

As we plant test plots of corn and beans, do you suppose God reached down and made "7-Foot" a test plot of His eternal plan?

What does God see as He looks down on the "Community of 7-Foot" today? Does He see Love, Joy, Peace, Patience,

Gentleness, Goodness, Meekness, Temperance, and Mercy? I think so. I hope so.

"Otterbein 7-Foot Church" is now closed. "7-Foot Church" died Sept 28, 1997. I had my last sermon that day. We had 78 present. The "7-Foot Church" was buried Dec 28, 1997, but I hope the spirit of the "7-Foot Community" will live on forever. I know it will.

Edward E. Brock, Jr.
Galveston, Indiana

INTRODUCTION

It has always been my belief that Jesus always taught the Disciples and His followers, whether they be one or a group of five thousand, in the simplest forms and in only the words that all could understand, no matter if they were highly educated or if they could not read or write. So all the years that I have taught and preached in *God's Church*, this has always been my goal. Jesus said without His Father, He could do nothing. Likewise I confess to you that without Jesus I could not have taught you. I had a dream and in that dream Jesus said to me, "Gather your Sermons and put some of them in a book, and title the book, 'Grandpa's Lessons about Jesus.'" How fortunate I was because I only have one Sermon, and that is "Jesus." That is all I ever knew to preach. I hope my grandchildren and anyone else that gets this collection will keep them and read them and grow closer to God the Father, God the Son, and God the Holy Spirit. I have been blessed with many great friends and good neighbors. I have been blessed with a great family. God has truly blessed Blanche and me everyday for which we truly give Him thanks. Don't just talk to God; but pray to Him. I guarantee you God does answer prayer. God Bless you all.

CONTENTS

Where is *God's Church*?
(Matt18:20)

"Where two or three are gathered together <u>in My Name,</u> there am I in the midst of them."

Two can move God to get whatever they ask and agree upon in prayer according to His Word. Two can constitute a local Church, with God's presence in Christ. Therefore, where two or three or any number are Gathered together with Jesus in their presence is *God's Church.*

The punctuation may be out of place and the words, here and there, might be misspelled, but I guarantee you that the words and the lessons are according to the Word of God.

I have only one desire, and that is to lead you a little closer to the Lord Jesus Christ. My fondest memories are the times I spent with you and others at *God's Church*, teaching you God's Word.

Without Christ I am nothing. Without Christ you are nothing.

J-E-S-U-S
Matthew 11:28-30

This is an invitation to personal discipleship, the way to rest:

"Come unto me all you that labor and are heavy laden and I will give you rest." This is an invitation to all men, women, boys and girls. If you feel tired and over worked, any hard worker can find rest in Jesus Christ. Rest in your Spirit, mind, and body.

Jesus says if you are heavy laden if you are carrying a load inside you that is getting heavy, too heavy to bear, one that is getting you down. Jesus says, "Come unto Me, Let Me help you carry it."

If you are over burdened with ceremony of Christianity. If you are overburdened with rituals of Christianity…if you can't do the things required of you to be a Christian, Jesus says, "Come unto Me and I will show you the way, for I am the Way, I am the Truth, I am the Life. No one comes to the Father but by me."

Jesus is saying, "I am the way, the only way to God, why seek you another way?"

The news media and magazines are trying to dispute the resurrection of Jesus. Jesus says, "I am the way of escape of your heavy burdens."

Paul says in 1 Corinthians 10:13, "There has no temptation taken you, but such as is common to man: but God is faithful, who will not suffer you to be tempted above that you are able: but, will with the temptation also make a way to escape, that you may be able to bear it." But God so loved the world that He gave His only Begotten Son, that whosoever believeth in Him should have everlasting life.

God says, "My Son is the way." Jesus says, "I am the way. My father sent Me from Heaven for this purpose, I came for this purpose. I knew what I was doing. I came anyway, for you."

The greatest Saint can stand only as long as he depends upon God and continues in obedience to the Gospel, (The Good News). Jesus is the Word, The living Word; Jesus is the good news, come from God. Jesus said, "I can only do what My Father tells me to do, without Him I am nothing."

And my friends, without Jesus we are nothing.

Paul said, "God made a way to escape." Jesus said, "In Me you will find rest, I will lift that load from you, I will help you carry that load, I will show you the way. Take my yoke upon you and learn of Me, for I am meek and lowly in heart, and ye shall find rest unto your souls."

GRANDPA'S LESSONS ABOUT JESUS

Christ gives us three commands here:
1. Come unto Me. (Move Brother, Move Sister.)
2. Take My yoke upon you. (Stick your neck out for Jesus.)
3. Learn of me, know My Word, know My Way, know Me.

Christianity is a verb. Christianity is a religion of action, mind, spirit, and body. The dictionary will tell you that Christianity is a noun, but I tell you Christianity must be a verb. It is a verb.

Now Jesus tells us about Himself, what He will do:
1. I will give you rest. (How tired are you?
2. I am meek and lowly in heart. (Don't fear Me.)
3. I will share my yoke with you. (Stick, your neck out.)
4. I will lighten your load. I am not saying I will take the whole load; but that I will help you carry it.

My burden is easy and My burden is light. Jesus says, "Walk beside me, not ahead of Me, not behind Me, but walk beside Me. Let us share this yoke, on the way we can talk to each other, we can get better acquainted, we can get to know each other better. Let Me walk beside you and show you the Way.

Jesus says. "Let Me give you relief from your heavy load, your burden." How do you spell relief? I spell it J-E-S-U-S.

Jesus says, "I give you peace in your soul forever."
Jesus says, "I will show you truth, wisdom, Knowledge." Learn of me and receive these gifts I have for you.

Jesus says, "I will give to you an easy yoke, an easy obligation. I will give you a light burden, a light load."

3

GRANDPA'S LESSONS ABOUT JESUS

Are you treading water this day, and not moving forward? Are you beating the air as a shadow boxer, this day? Are you floating down stream instead of swimming up stream? A dead fish can float down stream, but only a live fish can swim up stream. Are you trying to paddle up stream by yourself? Two in the boat of life can go through any storm. Life is like a ship upon the sea. Let Jesus in the boat with you, He says, "Come unto Me all ye that labour and are heavy laden, and I will give you rest, take My yoke upon you, learn of Me, for I am meek and Lonely in heart, and ye shall find rest unto your souls, for My yoke is easy, and My burden is light. I am the Way, I am the Truth, and I am the Life. No one comes to the Father but by Me." How do you spell relief? I spell it "J-E-S-U-S."

Jesus came to lead you to His Kingdom. Jesus told the thief on the cross, that repented, "Today thou shall be with Me in Paradise." Jesus also came to lead the Old Testament Saints into His Kingdom. They too were waiting for Jesus. They were in a place called paradise. They were held captive there, still awaiting Christ to come to rescue them. After the crucifixion, Jesus went down to them, and liberated those captives, taking them to Heaven with Him when He ascended on High. Now when the Christian dies, He is no longer held captive in the lower parts of the earth, but he goes directly to Heaven, waiting the Resurrection of the body. Christ now has the keys of Hades and death.

Jesus is the Truth, Jesus is the Way, He is the teacher and the source of Truth. Jesus is the Life, Christ is the source of Eternal Life.

Jesus is our leader. We are His followers. In other words, being

4

GRANDPA'S LESSONS ABOUT JESUS

Christians we are to lead, yoked with Jesus not followers of Satan's ways. I keep telling young Christians today, "be a leader, if you are a follower of Jesus. If you are walking hand in hand, if you are yoked with Jesus, then be a leader, and be mighty proud of it." Boys and Girls today, you are leaders, walk beside Jesus and lead other young people. Set examples for them to follow. Do not follow them who are trying to lead you astray.

Jesus in His teachings says you and I must do something. We must take action.

First Jesus says, take the yoke of Christ. A yoke is used to hook two animals together or in this case two persons together, you and Jesus. One cannot pull by himself with a yoke around his neck. A yoke is used to pull together. Jesus said, "Let Me pull the load with you."

In Luke 9:23 Jesus says, "Take up the cross daily." The Gospels benefits are solely on the basis of personal choice and meeting certain conditions. Jesus went to the cross alone, we need not to go alone. Jesus said take My yoke upon you, I will go to the cross with you."

We must create a habit to follow regardless of the price, even to death. Not only when it is easy, convenient, or popular. We must be continually willing to follow Jesus. We must deny ourselves daily, renounce self-dependence, self-interests, and self-punishment which are contrary to God's Word or teaching of Jesus Christ. We must follow Jesus daily, not just for a while. Not just once a week but at all times.

We should take no thought of Life. Jesus said in Matt 6:25,

"Therefore I say unto you, take no thought for your life, what ye shall eat, or what ye shall drink, nor yet for your body, what ye shall put on." Is not your life more than meat, and the body more than clothing? Life is more than physical. Do we forget the spiritual side of our life?

Quit worrying, Jesus says, worry is sinful and produces fear. Worry is opposite of faith. Be concerned, but do not worry. You are borrowing trouble when you worry. You are creating trouble, misery, or death. You are creating heavy weights within yourself. You are showing disgrace to God, and that should never be in a Christian. You are tormenting yourself over something that will likely be a blessing if it comes. You are living like an orphan. I never thought about that until now, living like an orphan. You are creating mental cruelty to self and to others. Be concerned, but do not worry.

Come unto Me, all ye that labour and are heavy laden and I will give you rest. I am the Way, I am the Truth, I am the Life, and there is no other way. This is what Jesus said. All other ways are foolish, for whatsoever is going to happen cannot be stopped by trying to avoid, going around or worrying about it. If it doesn't happen there is nothing to worry about. If it does happen, be yoked with Jesus, because should adversities come, one will still be victorious by trusting in God.

Did you hear what I said? I said, "Should adversities come, one will be victorious by trusting in God."

Let us Pray: "Father, we have heard Thy Word. Your Word is true. Now let us go forward telling others what You have brought to us today. Let us show the world, the community, that we are different, we are different because of Thee. Let us go forth and witness for Thee. In Jesus' Name." Amen

The Big Night For Jesus

I come to you today in the name of Jesus. Father, lead us in Your Word this day. Put the Word in my heart that you wish me to say. Use me this day to glorify You. Amen

I don't really want to preach to you today. I want to talk to you as a friend, as a neighbor; but most of all as a brother in Christ.

Every time I walk into God's Church, I am amazed at the beauty of His Church, and that is good.

But when I walk in and feel the Holy Spirit that is what makes a Church Beautiful. My friends His Church is really beautiful today.

Blanche and I were in England a few years ago, and Blanche's cousin and I decided to go to Church in the York Cathedral in York, the northern part of England, a beautiful Cathedral and huge. It had a sign that read services at 4:00 p.m. Arthur really wanted to go. He doesn't go to Church too often, so we went in and sat down in the back pew. Along came two nuns, and they said, "You two gentlemen should move up to the front row." And since they called us gentlemen, we were sure they knew what they were talking about. So we moved up to the front row. We didn't know what to do, after we sat down on the front pew, so we said we should keep looking around and see what the others do and we will follow. So I looked around behind us to see what the others were doing and do you know what we saw? We saw the two nuns that told us to move forward, sitting in the two seats that they chased us out of in the back row. I said, "Ladies would you two happen to be from our church back home?"

Well God said to me then, He said, "You will never make a comedian, get back to My Word."

What is the first thing you do when you get up in the morning? Do you know what I like to do? I like to grab hold of the hand of Jesus, and say: "Lord, don't let go." I try to walk hand in hand with Jesus. Sometimes I let go. When you let go of the hand of Jesus you stray. You know if you keep hold of the hand of Jesus, you are more careful what you do, what you say, and where you go."

If we take hold of the hand of Jesus, what do we have a hold of? We have a hold of the hands of the man that led the blind man out of the town, and when He had spit on his eyes and put His hands upon him he asked him if he saw ought. The blind man said, "I see men as trees walking." After that He again put His hands upon his eyes and the man said, "I see everything clearly." (Mark 8:23)

The town that Jesus led the blind man out of (by the hand) was

9

Beth-sa'i-da, where, because of their unbelief, once before, refused to do another miracle, in that town. Beth-sa'i-da was one of the cities Jesus said, "one of the cities where most of His miracles had taken place, yet they repented not."

Because of their unbelief miracles wouldn't happen anymore in that town.

How about a church full of people that didn't believe and say, "This is the year 2000, Miracles just don't happen today, that was for people 2000 years ago?"

The same hands that touched, healed, blessed and yet the same hands the people refused to hold on to. Were they saying, "We got our miracle, now we don't need you anymore?" So Jesus led the blind man out of the city to perform the miracle.

The more light men have, the less excuses they have for sin. They had Jesus, the Light of the World, but lost their belief.

We are to hold on to the same hands that lifted people up in prayer, without wrath, and without doubting.

And Paul said, "I therefore that men pray, everywhere, lifting up Holy Hands, without wrath, and without doubting." I am telling you today, to hold on to these hands, the hands of Jesus.

Every successful Revival has the hand of the Lord Jesus there with them. Peter said, "And the hand of the Lord was with them, and a great number believed and turned unto the Lord (Turned, means to do an about face)." If you are the same as you were before you say you were converted, then you have not been converted.

I would like to take you through some things I have learned in the past years. Again I say I come to you as a brother in Christ, as a friend, and as a neighbor.

I learned that God doesn't really have to have me. There is always someone He can go to, to replace me. But I learned something else. I learned that I need Him. I learned that He could use me. God doesn't have to have you, because you are replaceable too; but you need God.

There are many denominations, many different Churches, Independent, Pentecostal, Charismatic, The Church of God, The Assembly of God, etc. Many Churches are getting into the unity with the people, the world, instead of the unity with Jesus. Many Churches are sleeping and they are getting liberal. It seems as though, just about, all Churches are getting liberal.

I don't want Jesus to find me sleeping when He comes. The Word of God means nothing to some people. We want God's promises without keeping His Word. We are going to get His promises. God keeps His promises.

Who is the first one you speak to when you wake up in the morning? It should be God. It should be God. Too many of us want to know God on the surface but not in the heart. Paul says you can be religious and not worship the true God.

Man cannot impart the Holy Spirit.
Man cannot bring perfection.
Man cannot work miracles.

GRANDPA'S LESSONS ABOUT JESUS

Man cannot save the Soul.

Yet the apostles worked miracles among them. How? By Faith. By Faith, and not by works of the law, or the power of man; but through the Name of Jesus.

We get paid for what we do. Jesus said, we get paid for what we do. Isn't that nice of Jesus? What does He say. Jesus says the wages of sin is death (separation from God). The wages of belief is Salvation (forever with God).

We don't want religion. We want Jesus. He, who the Son sets free, is free indeed.

I don't have another message. My message is Jesus. Jesus said, "As you believe, so be it."

I read an article in the paper a while back that said you should worship God even if you don't believe in Him, because He might be real, but if He isn't what has it cost you. Oh! That is scary, that is scary. This is not what Jesus is trying to tell us. That is not what I am telling you today.

God His Father said, "I am, that I am."

Another article said, "I am headed into Heaven, but I don't believe many of my friends will be joining me." Friends, we are obligated to our, so-called friends. What kind of a friend are you saying your friends are not going to Heaven? I believe some people that go to Church do not want their friends in Heaven with them. I asked you before and I will ask you again, "Why do you want to go to Heaven in the first place? Why are you not helping your friends find the way?

I don't want to go to Heaven just to stay out of Hell. I will tell you why I want to go to Heaven:

- I want to walk the streets of Glory.
- I want to walk up and down the hills and valleys of Heaven.
- I want to talk to Moses, and the boy that had the fish and loaves. Why was he the one that had what Jesus needed?
- I want to talk to Peter. A lot of questions I would like to ask Peter.
- I would like to talk to Harry Campbell, my neighbor; he was the one that took the time to set an example for me to follow. He was our Sunday School Superintendent and I said I just want to be like Harry Campbell.
- I want to talk to Jesus. Face to face, eye ball to Eyeball. I want to look into His eyes and see what Peter saw when Jesus forgave him. "The look of forgiveness."
- I want to sit on the mountain top and talk with my sons Steven and Edward and they can show me around along with their friend Jan (Lynas) Hinkle who was my friends daughter. They all went to be with Jesus at a tender age.
- I want to see my mom and dad, all my family. Did they all go to Heaven? I hope so. But only they and God knows. I judge no man, but Jesus will.
- I want to worship my Heavenly Father, even more so than I do now.
- I want to be with you, my friends, my neighbors, my brothers and sisters. That is the reason I am talking to you today, making sure you do know about Jesus, making sure you do know Jesus.

Now why do you want to go to Heaven? If you do not think your friends are going to be there, then why are not you out there telling them about Jesus? Don't say it is not your job. My friends it is your job. You are obligated to witness for Jesus.

Paul says, "I am obligated to both the Greek and to the Jew and to the wise and to the unwise." Paul says in the first chapter of Romans, "I am ready to preach the Gospel to you. I am not ashamed of the Gospel, for it is the power of God unto salvation to everyone that believes, the Jew first and to the Greek."

I believe the miracles of Jesus. I know there is only one door into Heaven. Jesus says, "I am the door. Jesus is the only door that leads into Heaven."

I know that the way to peace of mind is through Jesus Christ. I know that God seeks all men. I know that all men do not want Jesus Christ. I know that some of you just want a part of God, just enough to make them think they are comfortable. I know that Jesus heals the spirit, the mind, and the body.

Jesus says, "Come unto Me, follow Me. Walk, beside Me, not ahead of Me, not behind Me, take hold of My Hand, Let Me take hold of your hand, Let Me take hold of your hand, walk beside Me."

Jesus said, "You can do the works that I do." Jesus said, "Go and tell, do what I taught you in faith believing."

Is there a God? Is there a Jesus? Is there a Holy Spirit? You bet your life there is. Did you hear me? I said you bet your Life there is. That is what you are doing, my friend. You are betting your life.

I also know that you can't just be lukewarm to Jesus, for Jesus tells us in Revelation that He will spew us out of His mouth. That does not mean spit. Look it up in the dictionary. It means vomit. Jesus says you lukewarm Christians make Me sick of My stomach. Jesus says, "I would rather you be cold toward Me than lukewarm. You lukewarm Christians are hurting My Church. You are making them liberal."

I know that Jesus is coming again, and we had better be ready. Some of us he will call home. Others will be here when He appears in the sky. Either way, you had better be ready. I know that there are times that Jesus is disgusted with me. I've done wrong; but He understands, He forgives, if we truly repent, and are sincere. Trust in Him. I know that God is not going to force you or me to come to Him. He still gives us the freedom of choice.

But I want to warn you, that the time will come when Jesus will stop calling you. He will always be available, but the time will come when you must go to Jesus, if you want Him. Jesus will always welcome you if you are sincere and want to come to Him. He will never take the freedom of choice away from you.

What was the Great Commission? The Great Commission was and is, "Go in to all of the world and preach the Gospel, to every creature, and you shall lay hands upon the sick, and they shall recover. (Some people say that is not for today.) But Jesus said, "I am the same today as I was yesterday and I will be the same forever." And Jesus said, "They shall recover." He didn't say immediately. It depends on how you believe. Jesus said, "Let it be as you believe." Jesus laid his hands upon them, the hands that I am telling you to hold on to. And the Scripture says that they all glorified God.

Acts 5:12 reads, "And by the hands of the apostles were many signs and wonders wrought among the people. (And they were all in one accord, with Jesus, not just with each other)."

By the hands of the Apostles, the Apostles used their hands to touch the people. But do you know where the other hand of the Apostle was? It was in the hand of Jesus. I don't care how much you pray. I don't care how loud you yell to Jesus. You must have your hand in the hand of Jesus. You must be connected to Jesus. You must be in one accord with Jesus. Not just in one accord with each other. By the hands of the Apostles there were signs and wonders wrought because they were all in one accord with Jesus. You can be in one accord with each other and not be in one accord with Jesus. Are you listening?

I say I saw the arm of Jesus once. I saw the hand of Jesus once. It was around the waist of our son. Jesus had his right hand around the waist of our son Eddie, and His left hand reaching out toward me. Jesus said, "Your son is o.k. Eddie is o.k. He is with Me." I saw the face of Jesus at the same time. His hair was darker than I thought it would be. Yet it had a golden glow with it. His skin was soft, sort of olive colored, with no blemishes. An expression that would melt your heart. But the eyes, the eyes, are something you never forget. They were brownish. They pierced through you. They didn't scare you. His eyes were loving, yet you had the feeling that with one glance He saw your whole life with one glance. It seemed, His eyes talked to you. He

16

didn't have to use His mouth. Now I know what Peter saw in Jesus eyes, when Jesus was walking, on His way to the cross, He looked over at Peter, denying Him, He gave Peter a look of forgiveness. Jesus didn't have to speak with His mouth. This was not a dream. It was happening at Sunday school at the Church. It was April 2, 1967. While my friend Everett Bowman was giving the opening prayer next to me is when I saw this. After Everett ended his prayer, Everett looked over at me, and said, "All during my prayer all I could think about was Eddie, and I felt the presence of Jesus so strong." Now maybe I should not have told you, but I feel God wanted me to tell you to get my important point across tonight. I told all this to our minister here at the Church. Our minister made this comment, He said, "Ed, you certainly have quite an imagination." So I said at the time, I said I would never tell anybody again, but tonight I feel that God wanted me to tell you, You being my friends and my neighbors, my brother and my sisters. I know that you know that I do not lie.

Every time since when I read the scripture Luke 22:61: "And the Lord turned and looked upon Peter, and Peter remembered the words of the Lord, How He said unto Him, before the cock crows thou shall deny Me three times." I know how he looked at Peter because I know the look in Jesus' eyes, and Peter went out and wept bitterly.

The woman that committed adultery saw the same look. The men who wanted the woman stoned, turned and walked away, because they too saw the same look in Jesus eyes. After Jesus told the woman to go and sin no more, this woman was pure as Christ could make a person, and as pure enough to be the mother of any child. Peter became as successful in touching other men for Jesus. Remember Peter walked on the water after all this. He healed the sick. He had preached powerful sermons. It was from his lips that this sentence came, 'Thou art Christ, the Son of the Living God."

On a cold morning, when Christ was in the palace, and later in the court, being condemned to die, Peter warmed his hands at the fire of the enemy. Have you ever warmed your hands by the fire of the enemy of Jesus? Especially outside, You stand there, and rub your hands together. (Now to rub your hands together, you have to let go of everything else.) That is what Peter did that day. He took his hands out of the hands of Jesus. He rubbed them together at the fire of the enemy. At that time Peter became aware that someone else was watching him. A little serving maid and she said, "You are one of His disciples. A Galilean, you are a follower of Jesus. No, no, no, Peter said, "You are mistaken." Again Peter denied it and again the third time. See what happens when you let go of the hand of Jesus? Suddenly there stood Peter, shaking like a leaf, scared out of his wits. Peter was a coward.

Then Jesus came through the hall. Jesus crowned with thorns, on His way to the cross. In a blood stained robe, spit on His face. His face red from the slaps He had taken. He was on His way to the cross of Calvary. He would stagger. He would fall. He would crawl up the hill, to be nailed to the cross. As Jesus walked that day, He heard a familiar voice. He recognized it. He looked and saw a group, stopped for a moment. He turned, the Bible says, He looked at Peter. And that is the verse I chose today: "And the Lord turned, and looked at Peter and Peter remembered the Words of the Lord." Peter this look I'm giving you is a look I want you to understand. I forgive you Peter. A look I want you to remember. I forgive you for deserting Me. I forgive you for denying Me. I think it was a look of forgiveness, a look of pardon, a look of understanding. Now this broke Peter's heart. Great tears ran out of Peter's eyes and down Peter's cheeks.

It was the look of the sweetest forgiveness that Peter had ever seen. Now Peter really knew Jesus. Really knew what Jesus had been teaching him. Now Peter realizes, he had let loose of Jesus, he had let loose of the hand of Jesus.

You and I say that we wouldn't have deserted Jesus, like Peter did. But we have. We have. People do the same thing today. We too, drop the hand of Jesus, and turn away at times. And Peter wept bitterly. Peter repented.

I might ask you if you remember the day that you really found Jesus? What the difference it makes to your living. What difference does it make in your life, with you living with Jesus and when you were living without Jesus?

Hey! Peter was human, the same as you and me. The way of the world got to Peter. Peter then reached out to Jesus. When their eyes met, their souls met at the same time, and Peter rededicated himself to Jesus. From that time on, I don't believe Peter ever left Jesus' side.

Look to Jesus. What do you see in Him? What does He see in you? Jesus says, "If you repent, I forgive you." "I am the Son of God." "Work with Me," Jesus says, "We will spend eternity together." But most of all He says, "If you have done wrong, repent. Look at Me, I will forgive you."

GRANDPA'S LESSONS ABOUT JESUS

I know there are times that God is dissatisfied with me, but He understands me. We must put our trust in Him as Peter did. God is not going to force me or force you to come to Him. But He understands us as He understood Peter. He gives us the freedom of choice, the same as He gave Peter. I also know that Jesus keeps knocking at your heart, and we must open the door. But I also know that we can knock at Jesus' door and He will open it to us.

<u>Now this is important</u>. I know there is a time when Jesus will quit knocking, but thank God there is no time when we can't knock on His door. (Only after death and then it is too late.)

Don't wait until tomorrow or next year.
Judas said, "One time won't hurt."
Peter said, "I won't deny you Lord."
Moses said, "Send someone else."
Thomas said, "I doubt it."
Rich man said, "I can't give up what stands between me and God."

God said, "These are the Words of my beloved Son, Hear ye Him, Hear ye Him."

I am only up here talking to you because I love each and every one of you. I know no other message, except Jesus Christ. I am not saying, that you are not saved. I'm asking you to come for a closer walk with Jesus. If you just want a touch, we will touch; lay a hand upon you, representing the Holy Spirit. Maybe just come and say, thank-you Jesus, then return to your pew. Maybe just say I love you, Jesus. Then, go and sit down.

GRANDPA'S LESSONS ABOUT JESUS

I just want you to come to Jesus. I want you to come believing. The touch of the Holy Spirit will take care of whatever need you may have. If you come, repent, and believe. Praise God it's free. Jesus has already paid the price, up on The Cross of Calvary. Praise His holy name. Praise you Jesus.

Now leave here today, not alone, but walking hand in hand with Jesus.

Who is This One Called Jesus?

Matthew 3:16-17: "And Jesus when He was baptized came up out of the water, and lo the heavens were opened unto him, and lo a voice from Heaven saying, 'This is My Beloved Son, in whom I am well pleased.'"

We are celebrating Jesus birthday on December 25 every year. Most of the so-called Christians in the world celebrate Christmas in one way or another, and most of us say we celebrate the birthday of Jesus; but still eighty percent push Jesus aside and give Santa Clause credit for Christmas.

But who is this One called Jesus?

God said of Jesus, "This is My beloved Son in whom I am well pleased." But let us go on to John 10:10. Jesus said, "The thief comes not but for to kill, to steal, and to destroy. But I have come that you might have life, and that you might have it more abundantly."

One day Jesus took Peter, James, and John and went up on the mount of Transfiguration. When they arrived there, Jesus was transfigured into His spiritual body, and there appearing beside Him was Moses and Elijah. And Peter having nothing else to say, He said, "Let us build three tabernacles, one for you Lord, and one for Moses, and one for Elijah." But God the Father hearing this said, "Don't put My Son on the same Level with Moses. Don't put My Son on the same level with Elijah. "This is My Beloved Son, Hear ye Him."

Who is this one called Jesus? Why did He come?

We find the two-fold ministry of the Messiah, Jesus Christ. We find in the fourth Chapter of Luke the 18th verse where Jesus was delivered the Book of the Prophet Isaiah. Jesus opened the Book and he found the place where it was written: "The spirit of the Lord is upon Me, God has anointed Me to preach the Gospel to the poor. He has sent Me to heal the broken hearted, to preach deliverance to the captives, and the recovery of sight to the blind, to set at liberty them that are bruised, and to preach the acceptable year of the Lord." And Jesus closed the Book and gave it again to the minister and sat down. And the eyes were upon Jesus, and began to say unto them, "This day, this Scripture is fulfilled in your ears."

Back in the Old Testament, God was in the heavens, and He created the heavens and the earth. At one time we find God was dwelling in the mountains. Remember Moses went down and he saw the fire on the mountain. He climbed up the mountains and He met God. That is when He sent Moses to free the Israelites out of Egypt. "And whom shall I say sent me?" Moses asked, and God said, "Tell them I am, sent you. The One without no beginning, the One with no end, that I am sent you." At one time God made an Ark and God's Spirit was in the Ark. Then man built a Temple for God.

Then God sent his Son Jesus, and God was in His Son Jesus. Now God lives in me, and in you, and all those who are to believe. I am the Temple of God. He lives in you, if you believe and have accepted Jesus as your Lord and Savior

Jesus came to minister to you. He came anointed to preach, and to preach the Gospel, the Good News, to the poor. This means He came to preach to the destitute, to the needy. He came not only to preach to the poor in spirit; but to the poor in body, the poor in mind. He came to preach deliverance to the captive in sin, those who were in captive in sickness, and in death.

He came to break the yoke of Satan. You know we are yoked with Satan until we get yoked with Jesus? Until we give ourselves to Jesus. Remember Jesus said, "Come unto Me all ye that labor and are heavy laden and I will give you rest. Take My yoke upon you and learn of Me, for I am meek and lonely in heart, and ye shall find rest unto your souls, for My yoke is easy and My burden is light." Jesus says, "Take that yoke off of Satan. Don't be yoked to Satan, be yoked to Me." Jesus says, "I want to walk beside you. Pull together with Me."

Jesus goes on to say in John 14:6, "I am the way, I am the truth, I am the life, no one commeth to the Father, but by Me." And Jesus goes on down and says, "I came anointed to heal, I came anointed to heal the broken hearted, the broken mind, the broken body and the broken Spirit."

In Acts 10:38: It is written: "How God anointed Jesus with the

Holy Spirit and with power, who went about doing good and healing all that were oppressed with the devil, for God was with him, God was in Him. He came to heal the blind, the blind in body, the blind in soul, the blind in spirit. Those who live in darkness." He came to heal the bruised, the completely crushed, not only those who were bruised and crushed in body, but also those who has a shattered life, those who were oppressed and had a broken spirit.

Do you remember the man that lived in the tombs with unclean spirits, which chains could not hold? In the mountains and in the tombs he cried and cried. One day he saw Jesus coming. What did he do? He fell down and worshipped Jesus. We see right there that even the demons knew Jesus, too. They recognized Jesus as the Son of God. They said, "Jesus don't destroy us, let us go into those pigs." Jesus granted their request and He cast them into the pigs and they went over the cliff and drowned in the water. The man with the unclean spirit was healed.

The man was healed and he said, "Lord, Lord, I want to follow you." But Jesus said he had something better for you to do. "I want you to go back to your own town, to your own people and tell them what great things the Lord has done for you." How many of you have told your neighbors, your friends, your family, what great things the Lord has done for you?

Who is this one called Jesus?

The Word tells us in the Book of Ephesians 4:8, "Wherefore He saith when He ascended upon high, He led captives, captive and gave gifts unto men."

GRANDPA'S LESSONS ABOUT JESUS

As Jesus promised, Jesus sent the Holy Spirit after He ascended into Heaven.

Who is this one called Jesus?

My friends, Jesus is the Son of God in whom God is well pleased. He is the Son of God that came just for you. He is the Son of God, who came to set you free from the bonds of sin. He is the Son of God who came to die for your sin, once and for all to set you free.

Some of the witnesses in the New Testament, after Jesus came, some knew His Name. That is all they knew about Jesus, was His name. Oh Yes, I know Jesus, I know that man. I hear His name is Jesus. Oh yes, I know that man, He is the carpenter's Son. He lives up the street there. Oh yes, I have seen Him before, I recognize Him. Yes, that is Jesus. Some of them knew Him as the Son of God. Some, as the King of Kings, and Lord of Lords. Some spoke to Jesus as He went by saying, "Hi Jesus" and Jesus would say, "Hello there." Some waved as Jesus went by saying, "Hi Jesus. How are you?" and Jesus would reply, "Fine. Bless you." Some knew Jesus by sight, some just by name and some in their hearts. How do you know Jesus? Just by His Name, Just by hear say, or do you know Jesus in your heart and Spirit?

I know that I know the devil picks on me and he picks hard. I said, "Get out, you are too late, because I know, that I know, that I know Jesus in my heart."

Some called out, "Jesus, Jesus, Thou Son of David, have mercy on me." Remember the blind man heard a noise. He said, "What is going on?" And the people said, "Why it is Jesus down the road, that is what you hear." The noise got louder and louder and Jesus got closer and closer and the blind man called out, "Jesus, Jesus, Thou Son of David, have mercy on me." And in my words, I think the crowd said, "Shut up, He doesn't want to hear the likes of you." But he cried out all the louder: "Jesus, Jesus, have mercy on me, O Thou Son of David." And Jesus stopped, and Jesus spoke, "Bring this man to Me." This blind man was not going to let Jesus pass by. He wasn't going to say, "Oh that is Jesus." He didn't shy back and say that's Jesus. No, he cried out, "Jesus, Jesus, have mercy on me." He cried out again and again. He was not ashamed. You know God will not move until faith goes into action. Jesus did not call this blind man to Him until this blind man released his faith? Then Jesus said, "Receive your sight, your faith has made you whole." He received his sight. Some people might say, well he just happened to be in the right place at the right time and it just happened; but not this man. This man praised God.

The Word says he followed Jesus. No he didn't walk behind Jesus on to Jerusalem. No he followed Jesus by following in the ways of Jesus, in the teachings of Jesus. He glorified Jesus. No, my friends, it didn't just happen. This is the Son of God. And the word said; all the people praised God.

Who is this one called Jesus?

Why can't we get people to come to Church and worship Jesus?

I want to tell you something, my friends. In 1980 I had a dream. At one time I raised chickens, ducks, geese, bantams, pigeons. I think I've raised about anything that has feathers on them. I had

27

them in an old brooder house I had brought down from the home place. And I took great care of them. I fed them well. I watered them well. I sheltered them well. They rewarded me by giving me eggs and fat bodies.

But I had this dream three nights in a row. I dreamed that one night I locked the doors so they couldn't get out. The next day I didn't feed them, and I didn't water them, and it was hot. After a few days, I looked through the window. Some of them were dead. Some of them were dying, and those that were alive were crying out. The second night I looked in again, more were dead, more of them were dying, and just a few were still crying out. The third night was the same. More of them were dead. A few more were dying. Just a handful were crying out for water. They were hungry. They were thirsty, but nobody fed them, nobody watered them. They were dying. If only I had taken time to feed, water and care for my flock, they would have lived and provided for me.

Who is this one called Jesus?

Then God and Conference assigned me as Pastor of Otterbein Church. I worked and worked and you all worked with me. We worked together. We grew and grew and grew. We praised God. We shouted. We sang. We praised God some more.

Then the other night, I had the same dream again. I saw the chicken house. I looked in the window. I saw the flock. They had all died. It was too late to feed, water or care for them. The Church died. Those who survived split up. Some today do not attend Church. Why do we not listen to God, when He talks to us?

GRANDPA'S LESSONS ABOUT JESUS

This message that I am telling you today is the message that God let me. Is this what we are doing to God's people today? Is this what we are doing to God's Church today?

I have told you this before. I hear some of you say you walk into the Church and you say you do not feel the Holy Spirit, then some of you say, "I walk into the Church and you feel the Holy Spirit." Why? I want to tell you why my friends. The Holy Spirit or God does not live in the church building. The Holy Spirit, God lives in you. You are the Temple of God. You walk in the church and say you do not feel the Holy Spirit. Why? Because He must not be in you. You do feel the Holy Spirit. Why? Because the Holy Spirit is dwelling in you.

Where is God's Church? Where is it? Matt 18:20 reads, "Whoever, wherever two or three are gathered together, in Jesus name, there is Jesus in the midst of you." That is the Church, my friends. That is God's Church. The true Church is not the name on the door. The True Church is where a group of believers meet together with Jesus.

Who is this one called Jesus?

He is the King of Glory. He is our Savior. He is the Lamb of God that was sent for the slaughter, for our sins, that we might inherit eternal life. You know Jesus wasn't sent to live, he was sent to die. How often has Jesus been waiting to put His arms around you, you my friends? But have you gotten close enough to Him for Him to do so? Jesus said as He looked upon Jerusalem, "How often would I have gathered you under My wings as a hen does her chicks, but ye would not." Jesus asks you and me today the same question.

GRANDPA'S LESSONS ABOUT JESUS

I have prayed for all of you. Sometimes all together, and sometimes some of you one at a time, in the years past. One day I prayed for a person's body. God took me through this person's body and showed me it was well. It was whole. The next Sunday I asked them how they were. They said, "I might feel a little better." And God said to me right then in my spirit, "But I made them well, I made them well."

Today I say to you, the King of King, the Lord of Lords, He cometh unto you today. You have to let Him in. Do you know who He really is? He is the Son of God. Do you really know why He came? He came because of you. If you had been the only person on earth, Jesus still would have come and died for your sins, that you might spend eternity with Him. Do you doubt this? Do you say, "I don't know what to believe?" Do you keep someone else from believing? Are you helping someone else to believe? You are why He came. Not to live, but to die for you.

The greatest gift you will ever receive is Jesus. The greatest gift you will ever be offered is Jesus. No one is too good, no one is too bad to receive this Gift. Have you received this Gift?

Do you know who Jesus is? Do you know why He came? Do you know where He went? Do you know He sent the Holy Spirit to dwell in you? Do you know He shed His blood upon the cross on Calvary, that you might spend Eternity with Him? Do you know all of this? That is the only reason I am up here today. That is the only reason. I care about you.

Jesus came to preach to you the Good News. You have heard the Good News today. I am sure you have received the Good News today. Jesus came to heal your spirit. If you have accepted

GRANDPA'S LESSONS ABOUT JESUS

Him as your Lord and Savior, He has healed your spirit. He has come to heal your mind, to take your mind off of evil things and to put your mind on good things. He came to heal your body. He came to cast Satan out of your body. He came to cure your aches and pains.

I have had an altar call every time I have talked to you. Right now I am offering you another. Will you come up and let Jesus touch your mind, body, and spirit. Just come up and say thank you Jesus.

After the service I am going to stand at the back of the church and shake your hand. The first one I hear talking about their aches and pains, sadness and all their problems, I am going to say to you: "Why didn't you leave them at the altar. Now Jesus says, "Why don't you leave your problems at the altar?"

Jesus says, "Come. If you don't know who I am, come, let me show you who I am."

I am not ashamed to stand before you today. I am proud to tell you about Jesus. In sports one team wins and one team loses. One half are winners and one half are losers. My friends with Jesus, everybody wins, if you accept Him. Do you know Jesus? Do you know who Jesus is?

God Prepared

I was talking to our neighbor, Charley and Judy, the other day. They had just ordered their little chickens. They commented that before the baby chickens came there were many things that they had to do. We must get the brooder house ready and everything prepared for them before they come. Doyne and Mary Alice have been getting spring lambs, but before they came, Doyne and Mary Alice had to prepare for them. I saw the farmers putting chemicals on the fields, preparing for their spring planting.

We don't do this by accident. We planned it ahead of time. Didn't we? We learned this from God. Maybe you didn't realize this, but it is true. Before God made man, God prepared for man. Things didn't just happen. God made them happen. God planned from the beginning, to the end of time, and into eternity future.

Sometimes man disrupts God's plans, as some people disrupt yours. We can do this because God made man with the freedom of choice. We are not robots. God said, "I want you to choose

Me because you love Me." You are free to agree and free to disagree. Free to accept, Free to reject, free to reach out, free to push away. Free to help, free to hinder.

In the beginning God created the Heavens and the earth. Why? For only one reason: for mankind...for you.

God said, "Let there be light," and there was light. For you. God didn't need the light. He is the Light. God said, "Let there be firmament and divided the waters." Why? Only one reason, just as it is for you. God said, "Let the earth bring forth grass, herbs, and fruit trees." Again, just for you. And the earth obeyed. God said it was good. By His Word God made the sun and the moon, light by day, and light by night. Seasons, days and years. Just for you. God said, "Let there be life in the waters," and there were minnows to whales. God said, "Let there be life in the air," and there appeared creatures from gnats to the albatross. Why? Just for you.

Again God said, "It is good."

God said, "Let the earth bring forth living creatures, and it brought forth cattle and beasts of the fields." For whom? For you. And God looked it all over and said, "This is good." Not bragging; but good for you.

Now see what God did? God prepared everything that man would ever need, before God created man. The same as you prepared for spring planting. The same as you prepared for the coming for your son or daughter.

Before God put man here, He put material in the earth to make that car you drive, for the livestock in your fields. Everything man would ever need between eternity past and eternity future. After God prepared, God said, "Let us make man in our own image. I have everything all ready for man." So God created Adam from the dust of the ground, and He looked down at His feet, and Adam was nothing but dirt. Then God breathed into his nostrils the breath of Life, the breath of God, and Adam became a living soul. You know I was just thinking. There, Adam lay on the ground, being nothing but arranged dirt. When God breathed into his nostrils, did God lower Himself down on His knees to breathe life into Adam? Without God, Adam was nothing but dirt. Without God you could say we are nothing but dirt. Without God you would be nothing. My point is, as you prepare your fields, gardens, or what next spring, remember that God prepared for you before He put you on this earth.

And God put you in charge.

So everything from the beginning of creation through out eternity is preparation. Why? Because God cares for you. The Bible teaches preparation from beginning to end, from Genesis to Revelation. He prepared it all for you. Everything God created was important. Everything that God created has a purpose. Everything was for mankind. Everything was for you. You are important to God. That is my point today. That is why God put you in charge. God said, "Man has dominion over every living thing that moves upon the earth." That is responsibility my friend. That is responsibility. At the end of the sixth day, God saw everything He had made and God said, "It is very good." (And that includes man.)

God gave you the best. God gave you His best.

GRANDPA'S LESSONS ABOUT JESUS

You are still in charge today. We still have the freedom to choose what we do and what we do not do. Mankind hasn't done too good so far, have we? We got all of nature off balance. We can't get along with each other. Countries cannot get along with countries. Races can't get along with races. Churches can't get along with Churches. Even so called Christians can't get along with Christians

Now God said, "I must do something different. So I will send My Son. Certainly they will listen to Him. I will send a fore-runner of My Son. I will prepare for My Son. So God prepared for John the Baptist to be born from the priest Zach-ar-ias and his wife Elizabeth.

And John the Baptist was born. Why? An angel said, "He shall be great in the sight of the Lord. And be filled with the Holy Spirit and many of the children of Israel shall he turn to the Lord?

God prepared the world for mankind. Now John is coming before mankind in the spirit of Elijah. Now John came to ready the people for the coming of Lord, Jesus Christ. John was the forerunner of Jesus. John said, "I have come to prepare mankind for the coming of the Son of God."

I want you to follow me now in my train of thought. In the beginning God prepared the earth for mankind. Now John the Baptist prepares mankind for the Son of God. John preached, "Come, Repent, Be baptized, and believe." Isn't that simple? Then why try to make it so complicated. John said share, "If you have two coats, give one to one that has none." Share. "He that has meat let him do likewise. John said, "Listen to me, I indeed baptize with water, but One mightier than I cometh. I'm not even worthy to loosen his shoes. He will baptize you with the Holy Ghost and Fire. John said, "You ask me if I am the Christ? No I come to prepare for the coming of the Christ."

Jesus came from Nazareth to Galilee, and was baptized in the River Jordan. And straightway coming up out of the water He saw the Heavens open up, and the Spirit like a Dove descending upon Him; and there came a voice from Heaven saying, "Thou art My beloved Son in whom I am well pleased."

Are you getting my train of thought? Everything from the beginning was for mankind; everything from the beginning was preparation. God prepared the earth for mankind. Now John prepared mankind for the Son of God.

Now what is Jesus going to do? Why did He come? Just for one reason, for you, for mankind. Jesus came to prepare, to prepare you and mankind for God's Kingdom, the kingdom of Heaven. Not only did Jesus come to prepare you for Heaven, we find that he went to prepare Heaven for you. Jesus said, "I go to prepare a place for you, and if I go and prepare a place for you, I will come again and receive you unto Myself, that where I am you will be also."

We didn't do too well with God's earth. But thank God, He is a forgiving God, and now He has prepared a New Kingdom for you. And I know just what He is thinking. He is saying, "This time I will remain in charge with My Son." I used the earth to find out the ones that love me. I'll bring them to Me.

Prepare yourselves for the Kingdom of God.

GRANDPA'S LESSONS ABOUT JESUS

This is what walking through the gospels is all about. Teaching you how to prepare yourself for the Kingdom of God by listening to Jesus and His Word. This is why Jesus came. You can forget everything I said, but remember this; everything God ever did was for you. All was for mankind. If you forget everything else, remember God loves you so much He gave His best, even His Son on the cross.

Jesus said before He ascended into Heaven, "Now you are the lights of the world. Go and tell, what great things I have done for you."

Remember the Samaritan woman? She didn't have to be told to go and tell. She was so happy with Jesus that she ran all over the town, shouting, "Come see a man that told me all ever I did." She didn't say come see a church. Not come see an organization. Not come and see a denomination. She did not preach herself. She did not preach Education. She did not preach rituals. She preached Jesus. She won a city to God.

When Philip met the Ethiopian who was hungry for God, he opened his mouth and preached unto him Jesus. Philosophy would not do it, but there is power in the Name of Jesus, and the result was that the whole continent received the Gospel of Jesus Christ. All of this happened because Philip opened his mouth and preached unto him Jesus.

It was Peter, who looked into the faces of that mob of Jews and told them about Jesus. When Paul was brought before governors, Kings, and Rulers, Paul arose and explained to them that Jesus rose from the dead. Educated as Paul was, He still was determined to know nothing except Jesus Christ and Him crucified. Christ is the Spirit of the Gospel, which speaks to God's desire for all people to be saved.

I want to ask you this same question again, why does a so-called "Christian" want to go to Heaven? Why do you want to go to Heaven? Why does anyone really want to go to Heaven? Do you just want to keep from going to hell? Just so you won't be tormented in hell? Are you just thinking of yourselves? Or do you want to go to Heaven to be with Jesus? If that is the reason, then why do we not want to be with Jesus now? If you can't get along with church people here and now, what makes you think you will enjoy Heaven. Let me tell you something. If you would seek the Savior, instead of seeking to be saved, you would receive something. Get in love with the Savior. Get the wonderful Christ in your life. Do you hear me? I said get the wonderful Jesus in your life.

If you are seeking to be saved, then seek a person, Jesus Christ. When I got married I did not receive a marriage religion, I did not receive theology. I did not join something or become a member of anything. I received a person. When I was saved I did not get religion, I already had religion before I was saved. Even those going to hell have religion. I received a Savior. I received a Savior. I became acquainted with a person, a friend, and a companion. His Name is Jesus.

When you went to school with your wife, or husband, you knew them, their name. When you began to court them you became better acquainted. Now after many years of marriage, you get to know them better, you know them well. Let Jesus move into your life. Let Jesus live with you. He will become more real and dearer to you, as years go by.

38

GRANDPA'S LESSONS ABOUT JESUS

You know Jesus treats all people alike. All classes of people look the same to Jesus, regardless of their race, creed or color. He loves everybody, He doesn't love all their ways, but Jesus loves everybody; but Jesus demands the same from all people. He demands obedience. He requires people to obey Him, to obey His Word. He did in Bible times and likewise today. Jesus is just the same yesterday, today, and forever.

I know one Man that can lay His hands upon you and you will never be the same again. It will pay you to go any distance to get this man to lay hands on you. He is a friend of mine. His Name is Jesus. Did you hear me? I said, "His Name is Jesus."

You know a lot of people, yes; but even church people don't believe all this. I am teaching you what I believe through God's Word and through the teaching of the Holy Spirit. Jesus said that when the Holy Spirit comes He will not speak of Himself, but He will take Jesus and show Him unto you, He will speak of Jesus. (John 16:13)

When I teach of the Holy Spirit, some will say that we should exalt Christ instead of the Holy Spirit. Brothers and sisters, the Holy Spirit will make Jesus a hundred times more real in your life. Jesus said, "The Holy Spirit will glorify Me." He will glorify Jesus instead of Himself. The Holy Spirit did not come to glorify Himself, but He came to glorify Jesus, the Son of God.

Now let us go back to the woman at the well. Remember she said, "Come see a man that told me all that ever I did." She preached Jesus. Some day you will stand before Jesus. Either at the altar to repent or at the judgment trying to explain all your actions. And you will confess everything that ever you did.

GRANDPA'S LESSONS ABOUT JESUS

Jesus said, "If you confess your sins and repent of your sins I will forgive you, I will forget them, I will erase them. I will blot them out." Jesus says, He will remember them no more. I will toss them as far away as the east is from the west. Think about that for a minute.

Come let me tell you about the One that I told all that I ever did. He erased my sins, He took them and threw them in the deepest sea. He destroyed what I confessed to Him, He set me free, and I am free indeed. I will not have to stand before the judgment seat, because Jesus forgave me my sins. I don't have to worry about the end of the world. I don't have to worry about dying, because Christ has set me free. This is why I keep talking to you about Jesus. That is the only message I know. That is the only message I want to know. I want us to learn together about my friend, your friend, Jesus.

Jesus, The Light
John: 8:12

Jesus said, "I am the light of the world; he that followeth Me shall not walk in darkness, but shall have the light of life."

John 1:1-14: In the beginning was the Word, and the Word was with God, and the Word was God. The same was in the beginning with God. All things were made by Him; and without Him was not anything made that was made. In Him was life; and the life was the light of men. And the light shineth in darkness; and the darkness comprehended it not. There was a man sent from God, whose name was John. The same came for a witness, to bear witness of the Light, that all men through Him might believe. He was not that Light, but was sent to bear witness of that Light. That was the true Light, which lighteth every man that cometh into the world. He was in the world and the world was made by Him, and the world knew Him not. He came into His own, and His own received Him not. But as many as received Him, to them gave He power to become the sons of God, even to them that believe on His name; which were born, not of blood, nor the will of the flesh, nor of the will of man,

41

but of God. And the Word was made flesh, and dwelt among us, (and we beheld His glory, the glory as of the only begotten of the Father) full of grace and truth.

Jesus, even before the creation, was the Word, not only the Word with God, but He was God. God created all things.

Remember in Genesis 1:26 God said, "Before the creation, Jesus was with the Father. So God created man in His own image, male and female, created He them." Adam was nothing until God breathed into Him the breath of life, and man became a living soul. At that time God made the body, mind and spirit alive and function together.

John 1: "In Jesus was life, and in life was the Light of men. And the Light shineth in darkness and the darkness comprehended it not."

Now then, John the Baptist says, "Here came Jesus. God sent Jesus down here. God didn't ask Jesus if He wanted to come but; God sent His only begotten Son." You know the verse, John 3:16: "For God so loved the world that He gave His only begotten Son, that whosoever believeth in Him should not perish, but have everlasting life." And Verse 17: "For God sent not His Son into the world to condemn the world, but that the world through Him might be saved." God sent His only begotten Son, that through Him, we might be saved. That we might believe. And here He came and the world would not even recognize Him as the Son of God. So John came to bear witness of that light. That light was Jesus.

Jesus came into the world and the world knew Him not. The

same applies to today. Jesus ascended into Heaven and sent the Holy Spirit to dwell within us. He left His Word, which is His Will (what is a will?). Man doesn't even take time to read the will of God, and they still don't know Jesus. He came unto His own and His own people received Him not. Remember in His hometown, not many miracles were done, because of their unbelief.

Remember in John 1:12-13 He said, even those that never saw Jesus, became the sons of God, because they believed on His Name. (Do you know what believe means?)

But it was those born not of blood, nor the will of the flesh (man) but those born of God, (the Holy Spirit). There are two different kinds of births. Even Nicodemus (a great religious leader, a well learned man), didn't understand. You must be born again.

In verse 14, Jesus was made flesh and dwelt among us, and we beheld His glory, the glory of the only begotten of the Father, full of grace and truth. Even Jesus told the woman at the well that the time will come when we will worship Him in spirit and truth. Jesus said, "I am the way, I am the truth, I am the life. No one comes to the Father, but by Me."

It came a time when it seemed as if the whole of mankind was headed for hell. But the Grace of God came through and He sent His Son, the Light of the world, to die for your sins, that you might spend eternity with him. You should shout praises for: "The Grace of God," "For the Love of God," "For the Living Word of God," "For the Light of God, Jesus Christ, his Son."

43

Jesus is the Light of the world. Jesus said, "As long as I am in the world, I am the Light of the world." This Jesus said when He was healing the blind man. (John 9:5)

Here we find that Jesus is the Word and His word is His Light unto you. Jesus walked upon the earth and was the Light, the Living Word. Jesus said that He is the living Word. Jesus said this. This Book here, the Bible, is the Living Word of God. Every word in here is the inspired word of God. No matter who wrote it, they were inspired by God before they wrote it. Saying that it is the inspired word of God is like saying God Himself sat right here at this table and wrote it.

So now, if Jesus was the Light and Jesus was the Word, then this Word is the Light unto us. Only this word here will bring us out of darkness. Now let us go to Matthew 5:14-16: "Ye are the light of the world. A city that is set on a hill cannot be hid. Neither do men light a candle, and put it under a bushel, but on a candlestick; and it giveth light unto all that is in the house. Let your light so shine before men, that they may see your good works, and glorify your Father which is in Heaven." Jesus says here: "Now I have come, I have brought to you My light. I have put My Word in you. Now you are the light of the world. So you can't go and hide it now. Jesus said, "let your light so shine before men, before others that they might see the good in you, that they might see the good in you, that they might see Jesus in you." Now Jesus says, "You and I are the Light of the world if we have His Word in us. The Holy Spirit in us."

I told you once before, I want to tell you again, we are transmitters of the Light. We are not reflectors. That is a big problem with some of us, my friends. Far too many of us try to reflect the Light of Jesus instead of transmitting it. The Light must come from within us. We are not reflectors of the Light. We are the Light. What did Jesus say? Jesus said, "Cleanse the cup from the inside first."

In Acts 9:1-9, it was a Light from Heaven that appeared to Saul and it knocked Him down. It was so strong a light, it blinded Saul and knocked him to the ground, destroyed his eyesight. The voice said, "Saul, Saul, why do you persecute Me?" His followers heard the voice, but saw no man. And Saul said, "Lord, Lord, who are you?" And Jesus answered, "I am Jesus whom thou persecutest."

In the same chapter a man named, Ananias saw the same Light in a vision. Now God sent Ananias to Saul, and obeying God Ananias went and laid his hand upon Saul and Saul received the Light that cometh upon him along with the Holy Spirit. It was the same light that Saul had seen on the road to Damascus that blinded him. Now it not only restored his sight, but also filled him with the Holy Spirit, as Jesus has promised to us all.

If you have received Jesus, and if you have been baptized in water and baptized with the Holy Spirit, Jesus says you can be just as much a light as Saul

There are two baptisms, you know, Baptism in water and baptism of the Holy Spirit. Water represents the death, burial, and resurrection of Jesus. The baptism of the Holy Spirit: Remember when Jesus ascended into Heaven, He promised to send the Holy Spirit. He said the Holy Spirit would dwell within you. He will teach you the Word and remind you of all things I have given unto you. He is the same light that Saul saw on the road to Damascus. The Light that touched him that made him see. Not only see physically, but also see spiritually.

Saul went forth straightway and preached Jesus. He witnessed for Jesus, for Him, and Saul didn't say, "Look at me. Jesus made me a prophet. Look at Me what I am doing. Look what I did for so and so" but Saul preached Jesus. "Look," he cried, "I want to tell you about Jesus, the One that saved and gave me the Light. Let me tell you about the Son of God." Have you received Jesus? Do you believe? Remember the meaning of the word "believe?" Believe has two meanings. One is "I think." And the other is "I know."

How many people come to God when they do not have problems? How many pray only when they feel sick? How many pray only when they have financial problems? How many pray only when they are down and out? How many of you pray only when Jesus is your last resort? Then we say, "Why does Jesus take so long to answer our prayers?" Why is God late in answering? You know God is never late. God is never late in answering prayer. God has his own clock. God has his own timing. We should say, "Yes, Lord I trust you even when I don't always understand you." It all comes down to one thing. You must trust Jesus. You must believe in Jesus. Jesus is the light of the world. Now you, you who believe are the Light of the world.

The Word is the Light of Jesus. The Word has power. If only all of you would come to know the power you have in prayer. Now before I close, I want to ask you one thing, "Do you know for sure you are saved?" You can know for sure. Shorty and I went down in the basement one night and Shorty said, "Ed, where is the light switch?" Jesus has given you all authority over darkness, because Jesus said, "You are the Light of the world, if you believe in Him." Do you know where the light switch is? It is Jesus, the Son of God.

Don't give up on Jesus. Jesus is never late in answering prayer. Just trust in Him. Trust in Him. Look for the answer. Listen for the answer.

Jesus said he was the Light of the world. Then Jesus gave the Light to you. Now Jesus wants you to go forth and light the Light of someone today or this week, in the Name of Jesus.

I heard a story long ago. There was a blind man walking down a dark alley carrying a lit lantern. Someone said, "Why carry that light, it doesn't help you see?" The blind man replied, "No, but it will help someone from stumbling over me." Is your light shining bright enough that no one will stumble over you?

Gracious and loving Father, we send this message with Your Blessing. We are thankful to be called your very own through the sacrifice of Jesus, Your Son, our Saviour. Prepare our hearts to receive your Light as we go forth into the world. Strength our faith and let Your Word guide, and protect us. May our lives be a transmitter of your Love and Your Light. In Jesus' Name we pray. Amen.

Your Duty
Ecclesiastes: 12:13-14
Romans: 1:14-17

Today I speak to you only one word, "Duty." I want to take this one little word, "duty," and I want to hang on to it, look at it, examine it, focus on it, and think about it. I want to tell you about your duty as a Christian. You know the devil doesn't care how religious you are, as long as you don't bear fruit, as long as you are not a Christian.

I have heard people say, "I am going to sit here until God's timing is right." "I am going to wait until God inspires me to move." Satan wants us as well as God wants us. Some one once said, "There was a day when it was a great honor, an exciting thing, to witness for God. There was a time when I could not wait to talk to someone about Jesus." Satan only wants us so God won't get us. God wants us because He loves us.

Another one said, "I do not enjoy the Bible anymore. I can recall when this Book was the love of my life, a love letter from Heaven. I could not wait to get alone and read from its pages

48

and learn the truths. It seems now, as though I no longer enjoy it. I no longer tingle when I read its pages. What has happened? I'd rather read a magazine. I'd rather watch television."

Another person said, "I don't want to go to church. Once I praised God I could go to church, but I don't want to go to church any more. What is wrong with me? I used to want to hear the preacher. Now I don't want to get up and go hear him. I don't know what is wrong? I don't understand. My prayers seem to bounce off the ceiling. I used to think the time of prayer was having a conversation with God, King of Kings. It was always a thrill, a delight, an exciting time, for me to come to the throne of grace in prayer. Now something has happened. I don't understand.

Now listen to me, my friends, right here we are about to separate the men form the boys and the ladies from the little girls. What you do when you no longer enjoy it, will determine whether some day you will rise to great heights for God, or backslide in life, outside of the service of God.

Worship is more than just attending church.

Listen, we are not supposed to read the Bible just because we want to read a book. We are to read the Bible because we are supposed to read God's word. When you come to that time in your life where the Bible no longer makes you emotional, no longer gives you a thrill in your body. When you get to the place, in your life, when you read the Bible out of obligation, instead of wanting to, you are getting to be a pretty good Christian.

Paul said, "I am not ashamed to preach the Word. I am ready to preach the Word. I am obligated to preach the Word. I am ready, because it is my duty." "I am ready because of what Jesus did for me." Paul had one goal and that was to preach Jesus. He was going to witness for Jesus.

When you come to that place in your life where you no longer want to pray; but you pray anyway, because it is your duty to pray. You are about to become a great Christian. You are not suppose to go soul winning on emotion. You are suppose to go soul winning because you have enough character to obey and do your duty before God.

Emotion is the poorest excuse on which to run a spiritual life. I came here today to instill into you the fact that you have a duty to win souls for Christ. It is your duty as a Christian. It is your duty as a Church. We need a transfusion in our churches; in the ways we serve God. Not because of emotion, not because it makes us look good in the community. Not because it might make our neighbor look up to us; but because it is your duty to. Because we are suppose to serve God. It is our duty to pray, to read our Bibles, go to Church, build the Church, to preach our sermons. Why? I will tell you why. Because God's Word says, we are suppose to, it is our duty. I am not saying that we are not, suppose to enjoy it. I am not saying that we are not to want to. I am not saying that we are not to, just for an emotion high. Good, dedicated Christians do what they ought to do, like it or not. It is their duty.

I can't inspire you to do God's work. Some people seep saying, "inspire me" to do God's Work. You do God's work, because it is your duty to do God's work. God and His Word will inspire you. Let me tell you when your Church will become a great

Church. When it is no longer real fun to break a record, when you no longer tingle when you meet a goal. Your church becomes great when it does all these things because it is your duty to do these things.

But you say, "I don't always want to." I'll be honest with you. I don't always want to either. I don't always want to teach every Sunday. I don't always want to preach every Sunday. I don't always want to visit the nursing homes and the sick. I think any worker in the church will tell you the same thing. You ask, "Then why do you do it? I do it because it is my duty. I do it because God told me to do it. I do it because I love God. I love Jesus. I do it because of God and Jesus has done for me.

You ought to pray because you are supposed to pray. It is your duty. You ought to read your Bibles, because you are suppose to read your Bible. It is your duty. You ought to tell others about Jesus, because you are suppose to tell other about Jesus. It is your duty. Emotion should not drive you. Obligation should drive you. It is your duty. It is your duty. It is your duty.

I was thinking of the thing I do in a day that I really don't want to. First I get up. I don't want to. I don't bounce out of bed. I crawl out. I don't want to shave. But, I do every day. I get up at 4:15 and go to work. I go out in the cold. I don't want to. Then, you say, "Why do you do it?" I will tell you why. Because I am suppose to. It is my duty to do these things.

For those that follow duty, God gives back the joy of doing it. Remember when you were first saved and wanted to go out and save the whole world. You found out you couldn't, so you quit. Your emotion ran out. Satan tries to discourage you and he hits you at your weakest moment. God looks down and says to the Holy Spirit. I wonder if he would do it if it were not fun? I wonder if he would pray if his spine didn't tingle? I wonder if he would read My Word if he didn't enjoy it? I wonder if he would go about preaching, if it were not enjoyable?

Then God says to the Holy Spirit, "Lift that tingle from him, take away that joy from him. Then praised be God, when you have proved yourself and you have proved to God that you will serve Him if you never tingle again, and you never feel that joy again. You will do what you are supposed to do because of obligation and not because of emotion. Then the dear Lord looks down and says, "Holy Spirit, give him back his joy, give him back his tingle."

Listen to me; you have no right to miss church because you don't enjoy it any more. You have no right to quit praying because you no long feel as if God is not listening, because you are not getting that tingle. You pray because you ought to pray and then you pray because you want to pray. There is a great difference between praying and just talking.

America needs more Christian people who walk straight, because they are suppose to walk straight. A man said once, "Young man, I am not so concerned about how high you can jump. My concern is how straight you can walk when you land." It is not what you talk about. It is how you live it after you talk about it.

Let me instill in you a character of integrity, honor, and decency. If I can teach you to do that which you are suppose to do. If I can get you to do the job that God has for you when it's hot or cold when you want to, or when you do not want to. Then you will have gained in this lesson, one of the greatest lessons you have ever learned since you have become a Christian.

I have learned during my lifetime that it is not because you have a bushy head of hair, or because you have a PhD, or because you have a majestic look about you, that you are a success. Rather, I learned that is because you obey God Almighty and do what God said to do, is what makes you a success. You must do your duty, D-U-T-Y, duty.

I found out that you don't have to be gifted. You just do what God says for you to do. Paul did not say, "What will you have me to learn?" What will you have me to play?" Paul said, "What will you have me to do?"
Paul said, "That is my duty Lord."
Paul said, "I am debtor, I am obligated to the Greeks, and to the barbarians; both to the wise and the unwise."
Paul said, "I am ready to preach the gospel to you, where ever you are."
Paul said, "I am not ashamed of the gospel of Christ; for it is the power of God unto salvation to everyone that believeth; to the Jew first and also to the Greek." "For therein is the righteousness of God, revealed from faith to faith; as it is written, the just shall live by faith."

Greatness comes by everyday getting prepared

Greatness is:
    "Not in a recital, but in the practice of weeks."
    "Not in the performance, but in the preparation."
    "Not in the pulpit, It happens in the study, preparing."
    "Not an "A" on a test, but studying for the test."

GRANDPA'S LESSONS ABOUT JESUS

"Not the World Series, but the Spring Training."
"Not the ball field, but on the practice field."

Ladies, if you are what you ought to be in the kitchen, the dining room will take care of itself. If you are what you ought to be in the study, your ministry will take care of itself. You know we are all ministers. You are all ministers, if not in what you say, then by your actions, by what you do.

Greatness is that person who says, "I am suppose to do it and I am going to do it." Duty is doing the job for God, day in and day out, great or small, easy or hard.

Listen to me, and listen well. If God has given you a position or taking His eternal Word written in Heaven, before the world was ever created, God's eternal Word. If God has given to you that privilege of teaching His Book to souls of this community, every time those doors are opened on Sunday Morning, it is your duty to be in your place.

Say what you want to, but if your name is on the Church roll of God's Church, every time those hinges creak, you trot your little self through those doors because it is your duty. Did you hear what I said today? Did you feel a tug on your heart, on your Spirit? I don't mean an emotional tug. I mean a tug of duty?

Today we should go home, not only with an inspiration to serve God, but also with character, with a sense of duty to serve God. Put God first, with a desire and a promise to do your duty, even when you do not feel like doing it.

I want to end this with the words of one of the wisest, if not the wisest man ever. Solomon said in his last verses of the book of Ecclesiastes: "And this is the conclusion of the whole matter; fear God, keep His Commandments, for this is the whole duty of man."

I met a Minister in Elkhart years ago that was just getting ready to retire. Rev. Lundy said to me, "I have had many Churches, and I never had one that never grew." I said, "Rev. Lundy, tell me your secret? Rev. Lundy replied, "I have no secret, I worked at it. It was my duty."

Now, I ask you. Will you go forth and do your duty?

Jesus Has Something Better

This is a story a preacher told me years ago. It goes something like this. A little boy came home from Sunday school and his dad asked him, "What did you learn today?" The little boy replied, "The teacher said, there was this big battle at the Red Sea, when the Israelites came out of Egypt. There were marines, tanks, and the army was there. They all came to save the Israelites." The dad said, "Son, I don't believe all that, I don't believe your Sunday school teacher told you all those things." "Dad," the son replied, if you don't believe that, you will never believe what the Sunday school teacher told me."

The boy changed the lesson because he didn't think anyone would believe the truth. Many are that way today, even some preachers, why do people change the meaning of God's Word, to suit the world, or to suit them selves? Why are we brought up as Christians and then we change to try and satisfy the world? We say, "Well God just isn't the same as he was years ago." I want to tell you something, my friends. I am not here today to satisfy you and your desires; I am here to satisfy God. Today I want to share the teachings of Jesus with you. I want to tell you what Jesus said. I want to share the teachings of Jesus with you. Jesus only taught the truth, even if sometimes, it is hard for you to believe. We say it is hard to understand. Why? Because we make it difficult. Jesus taught simple.

I want you to go with me through some of the teachings of Jesus today. First, I want you to understand I agree that the Bible was written by man; but God inspired every word, before man wrote it.

Jesus is teaching throughout the Gospels, "Whatever you have, I have something better for you." If you can believe, I have something better for you.

Sometimes we still act like Adam and Eve. Satan said, "Eve, I have something better for you than what God told you, eat of the fruit. It is good, it will open your eyes, it will make you like God." Satan says, break the commandments. Satan is a liar, was a liar, always will be a liar. That is one of his names. He has nothing better for you; only God has something better for you. That is why Jesus came. He came to show you His Father and that His Father has something better to offer, than what the world has to offer you.

John the Baptist said, "Repent, I have something better for you than your sins. You had the Law and the prophets; but I have something better for you than the Law and the prophets. I offer to you the Messiah. I have Jesus. I have the Son of God." John baptized Jesus and at that instant, God said, "This is My Beloved Son in whom I am well pleased. All through the Old Testament God sent His Word, "I am going to send My Son."

GRANDPA'S LESSONS ABOUT JESUS

And the angel Gabriel told Joseph, "And Mary shall bring forth a son, and thou shalt call His Name Jesus, for He shall save His people from their sins."

God sent unto you, His most prized possession, His Son. But we wouldn't listen. We still try to change His Words. The Word is Jesus. Remember it is the Living Word, the same yesterday, today, and forever.

The rich man asked Jesus, "What good things should I do, that I might inherit Eternal life?" Jesus said, "Sell all your riches and give it to the poor, and come and follow me." Jesus was saying to the rich man, get rid of all that is standing between you and God. Then come and follow me. The rich man, let his head drop and walked away from Jesus. I am sure, this is another time that tears came in Jesus eyes, as He watch the rich man walk away. If God ask you today to give up what is standing between you and God, would you give it up for salvation? The rich man's God was his riches. Our riches are in God the Father.

If God asked you today, to give up what is standing between you and God, would you give it up for salvation? Riches, pride, making a name for yourself, or for glory, would you give up anything for salvation? I tell you Jesus has something better for you.

Jesus went to His own home town, Jesus said, "Listen to Me I want to tell you about My Father, I have something better for you, than what you have." They said unto Jesus, "You are the son of Joseph, you are the carpenters son." Jesus said, "I have something better for you than the son of Joseph. I have something better for you than just the carpenter's son. I have something from God." But they wouldn't listen. The word says, "Jesus did not many miracles in His home town, because of their unbelief. (Because of their unbelief)." We can stop Jesus. We can stop God, from doing miracle, because of our unbelief. God hasn't changed. We have changed by twisting His Words into saying something that they do not say.

You know, you people here, treat me better than Jesus so called friends, and neighbors, treated Him in His own hometown. It wasn't right then and it's not right now. I am nothing without Jesus. God is everything.

One night a knock came on the door of Jesus, where He was staying. It was a man by the name of Nicodemus. Now Nicodemus was a very learned man. He knew the Word of God in his mind; but he didn't understand it in his spirit. Jesus said to Nicodemus, "Verily, I say unto you, except a man be born again, he cannot see the Kingdom of God." Nicodemus asked, "How could this be?" How can I be born again? Jesus said, "That which is born of flesh is flesh, and that which is born of spirit is spirit."

We either live after the flesh or after the spirit. What Jesus was saying to Nicodemus and to each of you, is, "I have something better for you than the worldly or physical birth?" Jesus says you must come, repent, believe, and then receive, to be born again. You must be born spiritually, let the Holy Spirit live in side of you. Nicodemus was thinking only on human terms. Remember we are not the body with a mind and a spirit; but the real you is the spirit with a mind and a body. The blind man I told you about some time ago. Jesus said, "What would have me do unto you?" They said, "Lord that we might receive our sight." Then

59

GRANDPA'S LESSONS ABOUT JESUS

Jesus said, "First you must do something for Me. Come unto Me. Then I will touch you. Then you must follow Me. You must ask, you must make a move, you must receive, you must follow, according to Jesus' Word. Jesus is saying, follow My way, I have something better for you than darkness. I am the Light. Jesus makes it so simple.

He simply says, "Follow Me, follow My way, follow My Word, follow My teachings. Don't change My Word. You will stumble all over the place. You will lead my people astray."

Let us go a little farther in the gospels. There was a crippled man who sat by the pool of Bethsaida for 38 years. It was their belief that every so often an angel would come down and stir the water. After that the first one in would be healed. Because of his condition, somebody would always beat him in. Along came Jesus and Jesus said, "Wilt thou be made whole? The crippled man answered, "but I have no one to put me in the water." Jesus said, "Rise, take up thy bed and walk." Jesus was saying, "I have something better for you." The man believed, obeyed, arose. He took up his bed and walked."

Excuses, excuses. Yes, we want Jesus to have His way with us; but, but, but, we say, this is 2000, God doesn't work that way today. The Bible says the Word is the same. God is the same. Do you suppose it is our faith that has changed? Do you suppose we depend more on worldly things than we do on God? I never heard God, Jesus, or the Holy Spirit, say "maybe."

Look at the friend of Jesus Lazarus who had died and was in the grave for four days. Notice what Jesus did before He called him forth. Jesus, first prayed, "Father thank thee that Thou hast heard Me." Then Jesus shouted, "Lazarus, come forth." What Jesus was saying was, "I have something better for you than the grave."

Now since the resurrection of Jesus, the real you, the spirit, bypasses the grave, and it goes directly to be with Jesus. That is if you have received Jesus as your Lord and Savior. Jesus did this for you upon the cross of Calvary, where He shed His blood for your sins. He has something better for you.

You know, I believe, Jesus prayed far more than He taught. Far more that He taught. Jesus prayed often. Many a time the word says, Jesus prayed all night long, and so hard he sweat blood. Jesus said, "I can do nothing without My Father." My friend, neither can I, and neither can you. We can do nothing, without our faith in God. Jesus said, "I cannot do anything on My own. I can only do it with My Father's help." When we discover this, we will have a great lesson. It is always with Jesus. Hand in hand with Jesus.

Moses, Elijah, and Jesus were up on the Mount of Transfiguration with Peter, James, and John. Peter said, "Let us build each a tabernacle." What did God say? God was saying, you are putting Jesus on the same level as Moses and Elijah. Listen to Me, "This is My beloved Son in whom I am well pleased." God was saying, "I have something better than Moses and Elijah. I have My Son. Hear ye Him."

Remember the woman in adultery? Jesus forgave her not because she had sinned but because she had repented, and accusers left feeling just as guilty or maybe more so than the woman.

You know God accused Israel of committing adultery against God. Are we guilty of taking the love we owe God and giving it to the world? Why? Why would we do that, when God has something better for you? God is a jealous God.

Jesus says, "Verily, verily I say unto you, he that believeth in Me hath everlasting life." Jesus is saying, "I have something better for you than the worldly life. I can give you heavenly life that will last for ever."

Jesus says, "My Word is Truth, My Word shall make you free; if you continue in My Word, then are ye My disciples indeed, and ye shall know the truth and the truth shall make you free." I have something better for you than lies, heresy, customs, rituals or worldly conversations. My Word does not change. It is the same forever. It will never change. Don't let people change it on you.

Jesus says, "I am going to send the Comforter, Holy Spirit. If you love Me, keep My Commandments, and I will pray the Father and He shall give you another comforter that He may abide with you forever." (This is the age of the Holy Spirit.) He is the Spirit of truth, whom the world cannot receive, because it seeth Him not, neither knoweth Him; but He dwelleth with you, and shall be in you. But the Comforter, which is the Holy Spirit, whom the Father will send in My Name, He shall teach you all things, and bring all things to your remembrance, whatsoever I have said unto you.

For ye shall receive power after that the Holy Ghost is come upon you; and ye shall be witnesses unto Me both in Jerusalem and in all Judea, and in Samaria, and unto the uttermost part of the earth.

GRANDPA'S LESSONS ABOUT JESUS

Do you hear what Jesus is saying, almost His last instructions. Start in Jerusalem. Where were the disciples? They were at Jerusalem. So what is Jesus saying to us here at God's Church? He is saying, "If you are at God's Church, then start at God's Church. If you are at Walton, then start at Walton. Start where you are now. Go and tell. Tell them that God has something better for them.

I stand before you today, begging you to understand that Jesus has something better for you, even:
  If you have more possessions, than any one else.
  If you are a good neighbor, and help your neighbor.
  If you have good morals.
  If you have the best wife or the best husband,
  If you have the highest education,
  If you have all wisdom,
  If you have everything, except Jesus, Jesus still has something better for you

Jesus said, "Without Me you are nothing." "I have something better for you. I have the best." Do you have the best? Jesus says, "come unto Me, I have the best for you." "Ask and It shall be given you, seek and ye shall find. Knock and it shall be opened unto you." Jesus said, "I am the door, and whosoever shall open the door, I shall come in. I will give you peace unto your soul." (Matt 7:7-8).

Jesus says, "Sometimes it seems like big things, like a mountain is standing between us and God." But Jesus says, "Whosoever shall say unto this mountain, be thou removed, and be cast into the sea, and shall not doubt in his heart, but shall believe that those things which He saith shall come to pass, he shall have whatsoever he saith. Therefore I say unto you, whatsoever ye desire, even when ye pray, believe that ye receive them, and ye shall have them." Now at this point most people close their Bibles and say, now I know it all; but let us look down a little farther where Jesus says before you get your prayers answered there are things you must do. First you must forgive others, then God will forgive you if you repent, then you ask for your needs, according to His Word. Have you forgiven others?

Have you forgiven others? You out there, right now, are you holding a grudge? Do you have hate in your heart? Do you have jealousy inside of you? If you do you will never have a happy family. You will never have a happy job. You will never have a happy life. You will never have a growing Church, if you haven't forgiven others.

Remember Jesus wept over Jerusalem. Jesus said, "O Jerusalem, Jerusalem, how often would I have gathered thy children together as a hen doth her brood under her wings and ye would not." And Jesus wept over Jerusalem.

Jesus still cries out today:
O Jerusalem, Jerusalem. Are they listening?
O America, America. Are you listening?
O Church, O Church. I want to gather you together. Will you let Me? Can you see My tears?
My children, My children, I have something better for you than self.

Jesus has gathered you a Church today, under His wings. I don't care what Church you came from or go to. I want you to stay in the Church that you go to if it teaches the truth about Jesus. No matter who you are. We are all gathered today under the wings of Jesus. And Jesus says I have something better for you.

I have given you the Word of Jesus. Now I give you the invitation from Jesus. If you need something better than what you have, then talk to Jesus. Don't live on worldly emotion, but on the Spirit of God.

The Most Important Question

If I was to put to you today, "What is the most important Question facing you today?" No doubt I would receive a variety of answers. Some would say, the threat of war, others the question of unemployment, maybe the balanced budget or perhaps the tax rate. Still others might say. The amount of sin among people in the world today might say is the most important question.

All these questions are very important, and it is our prayer that they be answered correctly. Still none of these is the most important question in the world.

The most important question facing people today was asked by Pontius Pilate two thousand years ago in Matthew 27:22, "What shall I do then with Jesus which is called Christ?" Far more depends upon the right answer to this question, than all other questions in the world.

What shall I do with Jesus, which is called Christ?

GRANDPA'S LESSONS ABOUT JESUS

Everything that is really worth the while for time and eternity depends upon a right decision about this question. If one does the right thing, with Jesus, which is called the Christ, you will get everything that is really worth having for time and eternity. Now on the other hand, if one makes the right decision regarding all other questions and makes the wrong decision regarding the question, "What shall I do then with Jesus, who is called Christ?" Then one will lose everything worth the while for time, as well as eternity.

Pilate asked the question nearly two thousand years ago, "What shall I do then with Jesus who is called Christ?" because he made the wrong decision, he is lost forever. Although he might have made the right decisions regarding many other important questions, he made the wrong one here.

Everyone who has ever lived is faced with this all-important question, "What shall I do then with Jesus Who is called Christ?" Thousands upon thousands have made the right decision and are now enjoying everything that is worth the while in this life and in the life to come. Others have made the wrong decision and have suffered loss in this life and eternity.

What does one get when we do the right thing with Jesus? In the first place we receive forgiveness of all our sins. The plain promise in Acts: 10:43 is, "To Him give all the prophets witness, that through His Name, whosoever believeth in Him, shall receive remission of sins." Every one who believes, on Jesus Christ, receives remission of their sins. Again I want to remind you, the word believeth, means: we know Jesus in our hearts, not just our minds, that we have accepted Jesus as our Lord and Savior.

67

I may say to you, or to a friend, "I shall come to your house Saturday night, "but before, I might get an emergency call that a loved one was sick or passed away and therefore I am notable to come. On the other hand when God says He shall do something, He knows the future. Nothing can surprise Him. Therefore nothing will ever happen that will keep God from full filling His promise.

So my friends, you may rest assured that if you believe in the Lord Jesus Christ, you shall receive remission of your sins. If the vilest sinner, who ever lived, believes in the Lord Jesus Christ, he receives remission of sins. He may be an outcast of society, but the promise is "whosoever" believeth in Him shall receive remission of sins. Remember that is believeth in Me, not believeth of Me. It is one thing to know there is a God; but another thing to know the God that is.

The forgiveness of sins depends entirely upon what one does with Jesus Christ, not upon our prayers performances, penance or promises. What ever else you may, or may not do, if you do the right thing with Jesus, you will get forgiveness of all your sins. Although, if you do the wrong thing, you will not be forgiven.

What a wonderful thing to know that God has forgiven me, and that He no longer holds against me the sins that I have committed. This blessed forgiveness is mine, when I do the right thing with Jesus. If you do the right thing with Jesus, you not only receive forgiveness of all sin, you also receive peace.

Isaiah 26:3 says, "Thou wilt keep Him in perfect peace, whose mind is stayed on Thee: because he trusts in Thee." The words trust and believe are similar. To believe on the Lord Jesus Christ simply means to trust in Him completely. Contrast this with what the Bible says about the wicked in Isaiah 57:20-21, "But the wicked are like the troubled sea, when it cannot rest, whose waters cast up mire and dirt. There is no peace, saith My God to the wicked." Today, when there are so many things to cause concern and worry, how wonderful to have the peace that comes by doing the right thing with Jesus. One who does the right thing with Jesus gets great joy. The one who does the right thing with Jesus Christ also receives eternal life. You know Christians are happier in poverty than skeptics and unbelievers are in wealth.

The one that does the right thing with Jesus becomes a child of God. John 1:12 states, "But as many as received Him, to them gave He, power to become the sons of God, even to them that believe on His Name." The apostle John thinking of this said, "Behold, what manner of love the Father hath bestowed upon us, that we should be called the sons of God." It staggers the mind and imagination to think of being a child and heir of God and joint heir of Christ, the One who gave His life for mankind. Do the right thing with Jesus and you become a child of God, an heir of God and a joint Heir with Jesus Christ. Do the wrong thing with Jesus and you lose your opportunity to become a child of God. You lose wealth. You lose the greatest honor ever bestowed upon an individual, and you lose the dearest friend one could ever have.

Do the right thing with Jesus and you are justified from all sin. Romans 5:1, "Therefore being justified by faith, we have peace with God through our Lord Jesus Christ."

When one does the right thing with Jesus, God not only forgives the sin, but also does away with the sin, so the believing sinner stands before God as if he had never committed the sin. To be justified means, "Just as if I had never sinned." It means God, not only forgives the sin. Blots it out. It no longer exists. I heard an old preacher say, "God has cast our sins in the depths of the sea and put up a 'no fishing' sign." Praise the Lord. Amen?

If you do the right thing with Jesus, you will be like Him some day.

First John 3:2 says, "Beloved, now are we the sons of God, and it doth not yet appear what we shall be, but we know that, when He shall appear, we shall be like Him; for we shall see Him as He is." What a glorious thought to have a glorified body like our Lord's. A body that could appear in one place at one moment and then appear somewhere else a few moments later, as He did to His disciples. A body that could appear in a room without any windows or doors being opened, as He did for Thomas; a body that could eat broiled fish and honeycomb, as our Lord did.

So I put to everyone here today the most important question facing man today, "What shall I do then with Jesus, who is called Christ?" Will you do the right thing with Him, or will you do the wrong thing?

What then is the right thing to do with Jesus? The right thing to do with Jesus is to accept, Him as He is. Accept Jesus as He is, and for what He is. What does Jesus offer Himself to be? Our sin bearer, that is what. The Bible says plainly in first Peter: "Who, His own self bare our sins in His own body on the Tree. Every sin that we have ever committed and all we will ever commit were laid on Jesus. For the son of man came not to be ministered unto, but to minister, and to give His life a ransom for many." His death on the cross paid for, among other things, the sin debt, that every sinner owes.

His cry from the cross, "It is finished," meant among other things, that the sin debt was paid forever, if we accept It from Him. The right thing with Jesus Christ then is to trust Him as your sin bearer, and as the One who paid your sin debt. Once you trust Him, all things promised to those who do the right thing with Jesus are yours. The forgiveness of sins, peace of conscience, unspeakable joy, everlasting life, and the promise that you will become a child of God. Justification and promise that some day you will be like Him. All are yours when you trust Jesus Christ, as your sin bearer and as the One who paid your sin debt at Calvary.

After you trust Him as Savior, there are other things you ought to do with Jesus. You should openly confess Him before men. The Bible says in Matthew 10:32-33, "Whosoever therefore shall confess Me before men, this will I confess also before My Father which is in Heaven. But whosoever shall deny Me before men, him will I also deny before My Father which is in Heaven." Romans 10:10 reads, "For with the heart man believeth unto righteousness; and with the mouth confession is made unto salvation. Everyone who does the right thing with Jesus Christ should come out openly and publicly. Someone once said, "Christians are like an Arctic river; they are frozen at the mouth."

My friends, if you have trusted Christ, then go and tell others about Jesus. Yes there is something else we should do with

71

Jesus. After we trust Him as Savior and sin bearer, we should go and tell other about Him. In Mark 5, it is recorded a story of Jesus casting the demons from one who had been possessed. And according to verse 18, the man out of whom Jesus cast the demons wanted to stay with Jesus. You see in verse 19, Jesus said unto him: "Go home to your friends, and tell them how great things the Lord hath done for thee, and hath had compassion on thee." And in the next verse, reads, "He departed and began to publish in Decapolis, what great things Jesus had done for him, and all men did marvel. May the Lord Jesus help you and me to go out and tell others what great things Jesus has done for us. Everyone here has a circle of friends. We can reach each one of them for Christ, by what you say and how you live. Live your life, in a way, that they might see Jesus in you.

These are the right things to do for Jesus, and with Jesus. Go forth and witness. Who among you will do this now?

The Choice must be made! The question is, "What shall I do then with Jesus, which is called Christ?" You say, "I won't decide today." Yes, not to decide to do the right thing with Jesus is a decision, to do the wrong thing. Jesus said, "He that is not with Me is against Me; and He that gathers not with Me, scatters." There is no such thing as being neutral. What will you do with Jesus? Neutral you cannot be. Some day your heart will be asking, "What will Jesus do with Me?"

Cleanse Thy Temple Lord
Psalms 51

This Psalm was by David the King of Israel. Samuel, a Prophet in Israel, anointed David. David was a Great Man. David had great respect for God not just now, but all during his youth, all during his growing up. Now he is a greater man because God had anointed him. So now we find the 51 Chapter of Psalms to be a prayer of David to God. After David had sinned, we see David was a murderer. David had committed adultery. David was a thief and a liar. David is guilty of coveting another man's wife.

David says, "Lord, have mercy upon me, God. Have mercy upon me according to your loving kindness. Have mercy upon me according to your many tender mercies. Blot out my transgressions. Wash me thoroughly from my iniquity. Cleanse me from my sins." David is saying, "Father I am dirty, God I feel dirty. Cleanse me Lord, please."

All statements in this Psalm are seeking forgiveness and

73

restoration to grace, seeking God, repentance, praying, confession of sin, and meeting other conditions are required of men who backslide. All scriptures require reinstatement with God when sin is committed.

Here in the first verse we have, "Blot out." Blot out, erase my sins. Confession is always a condition of forgiveness.

David says in verse 2, "Wash me thoroughly from my iniquity. Cleanse me from my sin. How could we be washed if our sins were not held against us? So our sin is held against us or we wouldn't ask God to do away with them. We wouldn't ask God to wash us. This is a requirement of God. David says I acknowledge, "I acknowledge I have sinned against Thee God, and I feel dirty about it." So I want you to cleanse me. This is awful, I feel miserable, and I feel awful in your presence God, for I am dirty. The sins of all men are not only committed against God, but against others as well. It is against our brothers and sisters in Christ. Yes, even against our friends and families.

Read Verse 5. We were born in sin. We were told in Genesis that we are all born in sin. Here again, this, a number of texts, that proves the doctrine of being born in sin. Now all these requests are useless if one does not need washing and cleansing from sin, again when he goes back into sin, into sins of backsliders. Backslider's sins have to be blotted out, washed, cleansed, acknowledged, and purged again. God must have mercy, be kind to, forgive and hide His face again from sins of a backslider if he is to be restored to God. A new heart must be created and a right spirit renewed in a backslider or he will be cast away from God's presence and have the Holy Spirit taken away from him.

In verse 8-15, requests were made and granted.

Make me to hear joy and gladness once again, he says. Hide Thy face from my sins. Blot out all my iniquities. Create in me a clean heart, O God, and renew a right spirit within me. Again David is saying, "Lord, I feel dirty inside, create in me a clean heart. Renew a right spirit within me. Cast me not away please. Please Lord; don't cast me aside, away from Thy presence. Please Lord don't take that Holy Spirit from me." "Restore unto me the joy of my salvation, the joy that I once had with Thee before I sinned against Thee." "Uphold me with Thy free spirit. Do this, O Lord and I promise you I will teach transgressors that way, and sinners will be converted unto Thee, because of my witnessing." "Deliver me from my sins O Lord, open my lips and my tongue will sing out loud of Thy righteousness, and my mouth shall show forth Thy praise."

Verse 16 says God desires not sacrifice. God's real desire has always been that there be no sin to make it necessary for sacrifices to be offered. God desires not sacrifice, else would I give it, Thou delights not in burnt offerings. The sacrifice of God is a broken spirit and a contrite heart. God will not despise a broken spirit. God's real desire then, has always been, that there be no sin to make it necessary for a sacrifice to be offered. This is God's desire. He didn't desire that we offer sacrifices for sin; but He desires that we sin not. If we sin not, then we need not offer a sacrifice. God wouldn't even have to offer His Son.

We are at the mercy of God as judge, and mercy must come, and it comes from what? It comes from His grace, not from the law. If we are to be judged by the Law, we would be killed, we would be dead, and we would die. The Law could only kill us. Check the Laws of God. The Law said, "David had to die because he was a murderer, a thief, adulterer, a liar, he did covet his neighbor's wife." The Law says David should be killed.

The Law could not forgive sin. By the Law David deserved death and would have been killed, so it could not forgive him. The Law could not give life unless perfect obedience to was rendered. Man would have to be perfect, and man is not perfect.

Now we see that the only sacrifices that are always acceptable to God are:
1. A broken spirit.
2. A broken and contrite heart.

A spirit that has said, "Lord," and a heart that has said, "Lord I am broken down, sin has torn me apart, I come to Thee now. Please cleanse me, O God, cleanse me and wash me thoroughly from my iniquity. Cleanse me from my sin. God will not despise a broken and contrite heart, because of His great compassion, mercy, and grace, which are promised to all, who are crushed and beaten to pieces by sin and by Satan's power."

Psalms 19:12-14:
Secret faults refer to those deeply imbedded traits that have not come to the surface or manifested themselves in life and conduct, and also to those secret things of life that one may be conscious of and may be hiding from public view. We do hide our sins, or at least, we try to.

Isaiah 1:16-18:
Wash yourself and make yourself clean. Put away the evil of your doings from before Mine eyes. Cease to do evil. Learn to do

well, seek judgment, believe the oppressed, judge the fatherless, and plead, for the widow. Come now and let us reason together, saith the Lord. Though your sins are as scarlet, they shall be as white as snow. Though they are red like crimson, they shall be white as wool. God is saying, "Let us settle the difference or put the matter right, that is between us. Such reasoning as this where both parties state their own case, will put an end to all other reasoning and questioning. The sinner will see his need and give himself to God, and then God will be just in cleansing him from all sin and making him His son. In other words, "Sit and talk it over with God."

If we will confess our sins, which are scarlet, a dye made of a small worm found on oak leaves in the, Mediterranean countries, and being double dipped n this dye, there was nothing that would remove it. It was permanent. Nothing known to man could remove this dye. He goes on to say, if our sins are scarlet, and if we confess our sins, they will become white as snow. Our sins have become deep dyed as the stain of a permanent color in wool, yet they will be removed as coloring from the wool, when it is restored to its original whiteness. This is how God can do the impossible with man. The Law cannot do it; only God can cleanse us from within.

Jesus said in Matthew 23:25-28: "Woe unto the Scribes and Pharisees, Hypocrites, for ye make clean the outside of the cup and of the Platter, but within they are full of extortion and excess. Thou blind Pharisee, cleanse first that which is within the cup and platter that the outside of them may be clean also. Woe unto, scribes and Pharisees, Hypocrites for you are like white sepulchers, which indeed appear beautiful outside, but are within full of dead men's bones, and of all uncleanness. Even so ye also outwardly appear righteous unto men, but within ye are full of Hypocrisy and iniquity."

Jesus is saying through traditions, through ceremonies, through rituals you clean the outside things of your life; but you never purify the inward man, from which comes the issues of life. No ritual, no ceremony, no tradition will ever cleanse the inside. Jesus says He must clean the inside.

This is the worst kind of blindness making people worthy of eternal blindness. They are blind inside, so therefore they are blind outside. If we are dirty inside we are dirty outside. Jesus is saying no ritual, ceremony, or tradition is going to save you, or is going to clean you. You can sin and come and join church, but if you no not repent and believe, you will not be cleansed. Only Jesus can cleanse you from the inside out. You can be baptized and not be clean. Jesus says; the only way to be clean is to come to His Altar. (Where is Jesus' Altar? I believe Jesus' altar is, wherever two or three are gathered in Jesus name, there is He in the midst of them.) Come to His Altar, repent of your sins, be sorry of your sins, ask God to cleanse you, and accept it, and you will be clean.

2 Corinthians 6:16 ask what agreement hath the temple of God with idols? For ye are the Temple of the living God; as God hath said, "I will dwell in them, and walk in them; and I will be their God, and they shall be my People."

When I had this country Church, we were having problems and I felt that God said to me, "Cleanse My Church." So a group of us started cleaning the building. Some of them were down on their hands and knees cleaning and waxing the floor. As we were cleaning the Church, I said, "Is this really what God meant when He said, "Cleanse my Church?" I said, "We are the temple of God, We are God's Church." I said, "God said, we are His church and He dwells in each of us, not in a building, God said, He would dwell in us, walk in us. He said he would be our God and He wants us to be His people." Then we decided, that not only the building needed cleaning; but that God was telling that we, as the Temple of God, needed cleaning also.

2 Corinthians 7:1 notes, having therefore these promises, dearly beloved, let us cleanse ourselves from all filthiness of the flesh ad spirit, perfecting holiness in the fear of God. Let us look at ourselves. We are all sinners. At one time we have all been dirty inside, and coming to church, attending church every Sunday does not make us clean. Joining church does not make us clean. Letting me baptize you doesn't make you clean. Coming to the Altar, and not repenting, does not make you clean. God says, I want to dwell in you. Look at yourself inside. I am not judging you. I want you to look at yourself. I am looking at myself. I am not looking at you. I am not judging you, but I am praising God, for drawing our attention to the cleansing of His temple. I just want you and God to sit here and look at your self.

God said clean My Church. Cleanse My Temple. Ye are the Temple of the Living God. God says I will dwell in them. But I want to dwell in a clean Temple. We have all sinned and we are all guilty according to the Law.

It is only by the grace of God that we can be saved. It is only through the grace of God that we can be cleansed.

God's word reads, "Draw neigh to God and He will draw neigh

to you." Look at yourselves. Cleanse My Church God says, I want to dwell in you. The only way that you can cleanse My Church He says, is to come, Repent, ask forgiveness, and believe. Then God will blot out those sins, erase those sins. Come, repent and believe. If we repent our sins: 1 John 1:9, "If we confess our sins, He is faithful and just to forgive us our sins, and cleanse us from all unrighteousness."

God gave us this message for a purpose. Cleanse My Church He says. We cleaned His building, and God said, "No, no, no not the building. Cleanse My Temple. You are My Temple. You are the Temple of the living God. God says, "I will dwell in you. I will walk in you. I will be your God and you shall be My People."

Dearly beloved let us clean ourselves from all filthiness, all filthiness of the flesh and the spirit. I want to be clean. Maybe you think I am being too hard on you today. Maybe you think I am being too blunt. My friends I want to tell you something. This week a 59 year old man I work with would have taken his pension. He thought he was healthy as you and I. This week they took him to the hospital. When they got him there he was dead. He did not have time to say, "Lord, Lord, cleanse my soul. Right now, you have time. God has put this upon my heart to tell you this today. Cleanse your Temple." Come, come to His Altar and by the grace of God, you will be cleansed.

We will go forth and say as David did, "Lord, we will go forth and be your witnesses. We will tell others what great things our God has done for us." We will follow Jesus all the days of our Lives. Amen.

All you need is Jesus

Paul writes in 2 Timothy 4:1-4: "I charge thee therefore before God, and the Lord Jesus Christ, who shall judge the quick and the dead, at His appearing and His Kingdom. Preach the Word; be instant in season, reprove, rebuke, exhort with all long suffering and doctrine." Now Listen, for the time will come when they will not endure sound doctrine; but after their own lusts, shall they heap to themselves teachings, having itching ears, and they shall turn away their ears from the truth, and shall be turned unto fables. Paul is saying the time is coming when people will not listen to the truth; but to bits and things of the world.

My friends, we are brothers and sisters. We are God's children. God has so much for us if we will but believe. I don't mean just saying it in mind; but in the spirit. Believe can mean, "I think." or believe can mean, "I know."

God's Word does not change. God's promises do not change. God's compassion does not change. God is the same, yesterday, today, and forever.

GRANDPA'S LESSONS ABOUT JESUS

Today I tell you the truth in Jesus, as Paul said, I do not lie I only have one sermon, and that is "Jesus." I preach the same message over and over and over again, "Jesus" "Jesus" "Jesus."

The Jews started the first church, but they were cut off because they rejected the teachings of Jesus. They thought their way was better. That is also what Satan also said, and what many people are saying today. We are living in hard times spiritually, and we need Jesus in hard times and in good times. Some times I believe we have hard times because we didn't keep Jesus in our good times. We find this true in the Old Testament. Now, do we say to God, "We don't need you, we have things under control?" We took prayer out of our schools. Going to church isn't important. We don't live like we are believers in Christ. We don't witness. Our morals are shot. We have disagreements and confusion. This is not from God. All this is from Satan. What would Jesus do if He were here in our place? Ask Him? I haven't seen so much confusion in churches in all my life. They are so liberal, it seems like you can do anything and no one says anything.

Jesus said, "I am the Light, now you are the Light." Some teach we are like the sun and the moon. The moon reflects the sun as man should reflect the Son. This is contrary to scripture. The Christian does not reflect the Light, but rather the Christian *Transmits* the Light. I can reflect the Light and be dirty inside; but I cannot transmit the Light and be dirty inside. Christ is all in all.

You know our Constitution was not built on religion. Our Constitution was built on Christianity. Today we are trying to define by the world's standard. My friends, it just doesn't, and won't work that way.

GRANDPA'S LESSONS ABOUT JESUS

Learn a lesson from this little story I read the other day. It goes like this:

This is a testimony of an old man:

"My wife has gone to be with Jesus. My children are all gone from home. My health is gone. I don't have much left. Come to think of it, all I have left is Jesus," and then he sat down. More testimonies were given, then the old man stood up again and he said, "Preacher, come to think of it, that's all I need, isn't it?"

All You Need Is Jesus.

In Exodus, the Lord God called Moses. "I want you to do something for Me; I hear the cry of My people in Egypt. I want you to go and set them free." Now Moses said, "Why me Lord? I murdered a man there. I can't go back. Besides, You know I can't speak. I don't even know your Name, should they ask me who sent me." God said, "You have Aaron, an elegant speaker. As to who I am, "Tell them 'I am' sent you." Notice, He did not say, "I was" or I am going to be," but I said, "I am" sent you.

God said to Jonah, "Go to Nineveh, those people are lost. Go tell them about Me. Jonah said, "Why me Lord? You know I don't like those people."

What is our excuse? We are the sons and daughters of God. We claim to be born again of God. We are joint heirs with Jesus. We have His power of attorney. We have His permission to use His Name. He has given us a blank check, with His name on it, signed "Jesus Christ, Son of God." Jesus says, "Fill it in according to My Word and My Father will honor it according to

His Word."

Like Moses and Jonah, we say, "Why me Lord? Now Jesus says, "Let Me ask you a question." Jesus asks, "Why do you call Me Lord, Lord, and do not what I tell you?"

In Mattew 20: 29-34, Jesus departed from Jericho to Jerusalem. Two blind men were sitting by the wayside, how long had they been sitting there? Maybe days, weeks, we don't know. Why were they sitting there? They were sitting there for their needs, alms, money, or food? That is all they could do. They were blind. They heard Jesus was about to pass by. They had surely heard of Jesus, His Words, His miracles. They said, "This is our chance, this is our day."

Now Jesus was nearing, and when Jesus approached, they called out, "Jesus, Jesus, Jesus, Have mercy on us Lord, Son of David." What happened? The multitude, the crowd rebuked them. Maybe the crowd said, "Be quiet, get back in your place. Hold your tongue, you are not good enough for Jesus. You are a nobody. Don't bother Jesus. He doesn't have time for the likes of you." I believe the crowd did say something similar to these words. But did this stop them? No. They cried out all the more, "Jesus, Jesus, Have mercy on us Lord." The blind men said, "This man Jesus is different. We can feel his kindness, His love, His compassion. We know He cares. We can feel it." Jesus heard, He stopped, he stood still and Jesus answered, "What would you have Me do unto you?" There before the blind men stood the Lord of lords, the King of kings. The Son of God, is saying, "What would you have Me do unto you. I hear you, what do you want? Tell Me." The blind men answered, "Lord, that our eyes might be opened."

GRANDPA'S LESSONS ABOUT JESUS

Some of us are blind spiritually. Jesus opens spiritual eyes to spiritual things as well as physical.

Two blind men are together. How long had they waited, waited for Jesus? How many times had they dreamed of this day? How many times had they talked this over? They didn't say, "Why me Lord?" or, "Why did you wait so long?" or, "Why have we been blind all these years?" or, "Why were you so long in coming Lord?" No they said, "Open our eyes, that we might see." Jesus had compassion on them. They *believed* Jesus could heal them. They believed Jesus would do what He promised. Jesus touched their eyes. What happened? The men saw. When? Immediately. There is nothing slow about Jesus. Hear me again; I said "There is nothing slow about Jesus." Speed your faith up to catch the action of Jesus. It is your faith that is too slow, not Jesus.

What did the two men do? The Word of God says, "They followed Jesus." They followed His instructions. They followed His teachings. They followed in His way. They lived it. Following Jesus is not walking behind Jesus, but it is walking beside of Jesus.

Remember the demon filled man that lived and walked along the tombs? Jesus healed him, cast out the demons. Then the healed man begged to follow Jesus physically? Jesus said, "No I want you to follow me by going back to your home. Go back to your home and your town and tell them, what good things the Lord has done for thee."

How long has it been since you have told anyone what great things the Lord has done for you?

GRANDPA'S LESSONS ABOUT JESUS

The blind men could have listened to the crowd. They could have listened to the world and let Jesus pass them by. But they didn't. Instead they called out: "Jesus, Jesus." and Jesus answered, "What would you have me do unto you?" What would you have done, if the crowd told you to be quiet? That is what the world is doing today.

How many times have you let the crowd push you back? How many times have you let Jesus pass you by? Jesus was going from Jericho to Jerusalem. The last time Jesus would pass by that way. Last chance, but they didn't know it. Jesus was on His way to the cross.

Today, are we letting Jesus, pass by, you and me? Jesus is not passing us by today. Jesus says, "Lo, I am with you always." Today Jesus stands here, hearing you call out: "Jesus, Jesus."

Jesus is surely here, just as plain as He was that day, on the Jericho road. You can't see Him; but neither could the blind men. They felt Jesus though and they heard Him. Listen to Jesus today.

Jesus hears you calling. Jesus is answering: "I told you I would be with you. What would you have me to do unto you?" There is nothing that Jesus cannot do. There is nothing that Jesus will not do, if it is according to His Word, in faith and believing.

Jesus is saying, "What do you want me to do for you?" What is happening? We are killing our babies. Television is full of hatred and crime. We have low morals. But Jesus still cries out unto us, "What would you have me do unto you?" We let the world drown out our cries of "Jesus, Jesus, Jesus." Yell above the

crowd. As these blind men did. Say, "Lord, Lord, I want to see."
All you need is Jesus.

What is Truth?

One of the oldest questions ever asked was asked from the beginning of time and the same question is asked today. The question is "What is Truth?"

John 18:38 Pilate saith unto Jesus, "What is truth?" and when he had said this, he went out unto them and saith, "I find in Him no fault." They did not want Pilate to judge Jesus, but to execute the sentence, that was illegally passed. Pilate was not willing to execute a man whom he had not tried and who was not guilty, so offered to turn Jesus over to them for execution.

Pilate said, "It is not lawful for us to put any man to death. This was another sin of the Jews. They had the power to stone anyone breaking their law; but in this case they lied, and fearing the people, determined to raise the plea of rebellion against Caesar, throwing the responsibility of the Lord's death upon Pilate.

Jesus had to die by crucifixion to fulfill prophecy. Jews did not crucify and they had no power to do so with criminals that were accused of crimes against the state, so they intimidated Pilate by accusing Jesus of not being a friend of Caesar, if he let Jesus go.

Pilate said, "Art Thou, the King of the Jews?" Jesus answered, "Did My enemies tell you this, or do you have any suspicion of Me, that you ask the question?" Now, Pilate was thinking, "If You do not profess to be King of the Jews, what have you done that they desire your life?"

Verse 37 Jesus is saying, "I was born to be a King and I came into the world to be a witness of the truth. All who are of the truth hear and obey Me."

Then Pilate asked Jesus another question: "What is truth?" Pilate, no doubt was confused with all the religions and philosophies clamoring for recognition. He did not stay to get an answer and in this, he is like millions today, who do not honestly seek to know truth, but follow every wind of doctrine that comes along. Christ is the Truth and anyone who finds Him and obeys Him will know the Truth.

I can stand here and run down every religion all day. I can stand here and find fault with every denomination. Then, that will never answer the question, "What is Truth?"

Pilate said, "I find no fault in Him." Pilate declares the innocence of Christ as to treason. Poor Pilate, he asked Jesus a very important question, "What is Truth?" But Pilate doesn't stay around to hear the answer.

Then the crowd is offered a choice: "Jesus or Barabbas." But ye have a custom that I should release unto you one at the

Passover. Will ye, therefore, that I release unto you the King of the Jews?"

Then they all again cried out, saying, "Not this man, but Barbarbas!" Now Barabbas was a robber.

Does, who I am, make truth? Does what I am, make truth? Does what I do, make truth? Does what I believe, make truth? Does what I say, Make truth? Does what I preach or what I teach, make truth? Jesus said in John 14:6, "I am the Way, the Truth, and the Life; no man cometh unto the Father, but by Me. I am the door that leads into Heaven."

Pilate was confused, people today get confused, children today, get confused. Nations of the world today get confused. People in our country get confused about our government, as I told you before, the government and the constitution was built upon Christianity, not religion.

Confusion comes from Satan. Truth comes from Jesus.

John 1:14 reads, "and the Word was made flesh, and dwelt among us, and we beheld His Glory, the Glory of the only begotten of the Father, full of Grace and Truth." John bare witness of Jesus, and cried saying, " this was He of whom I spake, He that cometh after is preferred before me; for He was before Me. And of His fullness have all we received, and grace for grace. For the Law was given by Moses, but Grace and Truth came by Jesus Christ."

"God's Word is Truth."

John 4:24 God is spirit, and they that worship Him must worship Him in Spirit and Truth.

John 8:32 Jesus said, "If ye continue in My Word, then are ye My disciples, indeed; and ye shall know the Truth, and the Truth shall make you free."

John 16:12 "I have yet many things to say unto you, but ye cannot hear them now."

John 16:13 "How be it when He, the Spirit of Truth, is come, He will guide you into all Truth, for He shall not speak of Himself, but whatsoever He shall hear, that shall He speak, and He will show you things to come."

Acts 1:4-5 "But wait for the promise of the Father, which saith He, ye have heard of Me. For John truly baptized with water; but Ye shall baptize with the Holy Spirit, not many days hence."

Acts1: 4-8 "But ye shall receive power, after that the Holy Spirit is come upon you, and ye shall be witnesses unto Me both in Jerusalem and Judea, and unto the uttermost part of the earth, and ye shall be witnesses." Ye shall tell the Truth. Then Jesus was taken up and a cloud received Him out of their sight.

As Jesus ascended up into Heaven, the angels standing there said, "Why stand ye gazing up into Heaven? This same Jesus, which is taken up from you into Heaven, shall so come in like Manner as ye have seen Him go into Heaven."

What is Truth? God is Truth. Jesus is Truth. God's Word is Truth. The Word of God is truth and Jesus was the Living Word. The Holy Spirit is Truth.

You are truth, if you are baptized with the Holy Spirit. You are Truth, if you are filled with the Word of God. If you are a witness for Jesus, you are truth.

Truth never changes. God never changes. God said, "I am, that I am." He isn't saying He was or He is going to be but God said, "I am." He is the same yesterday, today, and forever.

"What is Truth?" Pilate said, "What is Truth?" My children said, "What is Truth?" People today are saying, "What is Truth?"

Pilate was no doubt, confused by all the religions and Philosophies of his time. If he was so confused, people today are even more so. Pilate didn't stay to find the answer, although he really wanted to know the answer.

Jesus is the Truth, and anyone who finds Him and obeys Him, will know the truth, and the truth will set them free. God never changes. Truth never changes. Truth is the same yesterday, today, and forever.

The Pharisees said in Matt 22:16 "Master, we know that Thou art True; and Thou teacheth the way of God in Truth."

But people tried to kill the Truth 2000 years ago and people today are still trying to kill the Truth. People are saying, "It is all right if you do this or that even if it is not always according to God's Word." But God says it is all right if you doeth Truth and God's Word is the Truth. Rev 19:11- John says, "I saw Heaven opened and saw Christ upon a White Horse and He was called faithful and true. Also His Name is called the, "Word of God."

The Bible, The Word of God, is Truth. God, is Truth. Jesus, is Truth. The Holy Spirit, is Truth. God's Way, is Truth. And if you walk in the way of Jesus, and you let Jesus walk beside you, and let the Holy Spirit dwell in you, you are Truth.

GRANDPA'S LESSONS ABOUT JESUS

Jesus said, "The time will come, when Man will not worship in a certain place, or by a certain man; but the day will come when man will worship, where ever he might be, and he will worship in Spirit and Truth." I believe that day is here, today. Today is that day. If you can't worship God in Spirit and Truth, if you can't worship God anywhere, anytime, and if you cannot live a Christian Life daily, then come and let God fill you with His Spirit of Truth. Do it today.

What Would You Have God Do For You?

God told Solomon to ask, what he wanted, and it is plainly implied that the request would be granted. Those who express the desire to have God, say to them, what he did to Solomon, should realize that he does, and even more. If one doubts this, let him turn to the following plain and unlimited promises of God to His children in New Testament times:

1. "Ask and you shall receive. (Matt 7:7)
2. "Seek and you shall find. (Matt 7:7-11)
3. "Knock and it shall be opened unto you. (Matt 7:7)
4. "Nothing shall be impossible unto you. (Matt 17:20)
5. "All things, whatsoever you shall ask in prayer, believing, you shall receive. (Matt 21: 21-22)
6. "All things are possible, to him that believeth. (Mk 9:23, 11:22-24)
7. "Ask what you will, and it shall be done unto you. (Jn 15:7)

God is the same today as He was yesterday, and He will be the same tomorrow. In the Old Testament, two things God did for David. We read in 2 Chronicles 1:8, "And Solomon said unto God, 'Thou hast shewed great mercy unto David, my father, and

94

gave him a son to sit upon his throne in his place.'"

Here are two requests of Solomon, to God, First Solomon said, "Let your promise to David be established." Second, "Give me now wisdom and knowledge, that I may go out and come in before this people; for who can judge Your people, that is so great?"

Now let us look at Solomon's request, which sets the standard for all who desire to please God and be blessed by Him. It was for wisdom and understanding in the science of government to judge Israel, in true justice. He desired gifts that would best qualify him for his work and call in life.

Too often men pray for gifts, which they think will make them great in the eyes of others. They want to imitate the greatness of some other man and they are not called or qualified for that particular work. Their motive is one of selfishness and self-gratification. One of the great functions of the oriental monarch has always been to hear and decide causes; hence the chief desire of Solomon was to be his best, by God's inspiration, and gifts to judge great people and their territory.

God's promises to Solomon:
1. "I will give you wisdom and knowledge."
2. "I will give you riches."
3. "I will give you wealth."
4. "I will give you honor."
5. "I will give you all these things, as no king before you has received; neither shall any after you, have the like."

Solomon was one of the world's richest men. He had the

greatest honor from men of all ages. They came from the far countries to hear his wisdom and see his wealth and glory.

Two things Solomon was determined to do:
1. "I will build a temple."
2. "I then will build a palace."

God said unto Solomon, "Ask what I shall give thee." Remember that Jesus said also, a similar thing to the blind man, when He said, "What would you have Me do unto you?" Jesus said in Mark 11:22-24, "Whatsoever you desire, when you pray, believe that ye receive them, and ye shall have them."

Now Solomon received what he asked for. What did God think of Solomon? Does God think more of Solomon than He does of you? Did God answer Solomon's prayers and not yours? Why? Why doesn't God answer your prayers? Did He love Solomon more than He loves you? No. Do you really believe, as Solomon did? Thomas doubted. Do you doubt?

Solomon knew God. Solomon loved God. Solomon trusted God. Solomon knew God's Laws. Solomon believed. (Knew for sure.) Solomon didn't just hope; but Solomon *knew* God, for sure, and so can you. Remember Solomon was human, the same as you. Solomon strayed from God. Strange women brought in pagan worship. Solomon committed adultery against God. By this I mean that Solomon, took the Love that belonged to God and gave it to the world. Do you understand what I am telling you?

I want to list some discoveries of Solomon. This I read somewhere, I don't remember where, so don't give me credit for it. I did check it out and found it to be right. This is from Solomon himself:

- The race is not to the swift. It is to the one on God's side.
- The battle is not to the strong. It is to the one on God's side.
- Bread is not only for the wise. It is to the believer.
- Riches are not only to men of understanding. It is to the one with faith.
- Labor is not only for men of skill. It is those with obedience.
- Man does not know the time of his death. Death comes at all ages.
- Wisdom is better than strength. (Moses in Egypt.)
- Poor people are not appreciated for great public deeds. (God recognizes the poor. Man seems not to.)
- The wisdom and words of the poor are despised, nor appreciated. (Who are you to tell me what to do? This sounds like the crowd that tried to stop the blind men from going to Jesus.)
- A wise mans words are rejected by fools. (God's word is wisest.)
- Wisdom is better than weapons of war. (God's word is like a two edged sword.)
- One sinner unbridled destroys much good. A sinner can draw a good man to him easier than a good man can draw a sinner.

Solomon came to this conclusion, after he sinned against God.
1. Man's work is unprofitable, (vanity) without God.
2. Wisdom, knowledge, madness is vanity, without God.
3. Personal pleasures are vanity without God.
4. Great works. Riches and Glory are vanity without God.
5. Long life means nothing without God.

6. Vanity is a miser's life.
7. Vows mean nothing without God.
8. There is no justice without God.
9. Money and Riches are a worry and a burden without God.
10. Desires and appetites are never satisfied without God.
11. Don't be self-righteous. Only be righteous in the Way of Jesus.
12. Good conduct is vanity without God.

Now Solomon writes, "Let us hear the conclusion of the whole matter: Fear God, and keep His commandments, for this is the whole duty of man. For God shall bring every work into judgment, with every secret thing, whether it be good, or whether it be evil."

(I want to make this comment here. I believe the book of Ecclesiastes was Solomon repenting to God for letting Him down. Repenting to God for his sins. I might add, that I have been told by a few ministers that I am wrong, but this truly what I believe.)

And so Solomon repented to God.

The whole duty of man is to fear God, to keep His commandments. To prepare for eternity, in view of the fact that every work of man will be brought into judgment, even every secret thing, whether it be good or it be evil.

Remember in the beginning of this lesson Solomon asked God for Wisdom and knowledge? We see here Solomon did not lose his wisdom and knowledge, which had been imparted to him as gifts from God, because they became a part of Solomon.

GRANDPA'S LESSONS ABOUT JESUS

I think if Solomon could write to you today, he would write you a letter like this:

My Dear Friends,

Through my wisdom and knowledge I received from my Heavenly Father, I want to teach you a lesson. To you at God's Church, I say to you: No matter what you think you have, no matter what you think you are, you are nothing without God, You have nothing that God did not give you. God was very good to me. He gave me wisdom and knowledge. I used it for the Glory of God and He blessed me. Then I used it to sin against God and turned away from Him. But through the wisdom and knowledge He gave to me I was drawn back to Him, because I found that without God, the only true God, life is nothing. It is all vanity.

So to you, at God's Church, I Solomon, say to you, if you want your life to mean something. If you want your possessions to amount to anything, take God as your partner, take God as your Guide, for without God you will never be satisfied. You will never be happy. You will never spend eternity with Him.

You at God's Church, learn this lesson, and learn it well. I drifted from My God. I turned away from Him. I saw my errors, I repented, and God accepted me back. I Solomon, ask you, at God's Church, to learn a lesson from my mistakes. Please do this for me, that I may see you, and be with you in the Kingdom of God.

> God's Love,
> Solomon

Let Us Check Our Salvation

Romans 3:23: "For we have sinned, and come short of the glory or God." To start off with, we must know and confess we are sinners, before we can be saved.

Romans 6:23: "For the wages of sin is death; but the gift of God is eternal life through Jesus Christ, our Lord." You earn your wages. Divine justice is under obligation to give sinners their wages or be in debt to them forever; but eternal life is a gift, a free gift. We merit hell, but not eternal life. Jesus Christ alone procured it and gives it freely in all who believe.

Acts 16:30-31: The jailer, who had been watching after Paul and Silas, said, "What must I do to be saved?" And they answered, "Believe on the Lord Jesus Christ, and thou shalt be saved, and thy house." Then they spake unto him the word of the Lord.

This is the simple way to get saved, when one is under conviction of sin, and as desperate as this man was. It is not a formal confession that is uttered here, but that kind of faith that will surrender all to God and believe, with the heart, the truth that is known. A formal mental acceptance of Jesus, at any time or place, will not save the soul. It must be a genuine heart felt transaction of repentance and faith. It would be vain to ask a man to do this who was not willing and ready to do it and who had not been convicted of sin and knew his need.

The Word of God was preached to the whole house and the way of salvation was made clear. All in the house did accept the Gospel and were baptized.

Ephesians 2:8-9: "For by grace are ye saved through faith; and that not of yourselves; it is the gift of God. Not of works, lest any man should boast, for we are His workmanship, created in Christ Jesus unto good works, which God hath before, ordained, that we should walk in them." This is a simple statement of how men are resurrected spiritually from death in sins. We are created by God to be His workmen. Through salvation, God is preparing us for good works, which He expects them to do, and it is our duty to do them.

Romans 10:9-13: "That if thou shalt confess, with thy mouth the Lord Jesus and shalt believe in thine heart, that God hath raised Jesus from the dead, thou shall be saved. For with the heart man believeth unto righteousness; and with the mouth, confession is made unto salvation. For the scripture saith, who so ever believeth on Him shall not be ashamed. For there is no difference between the Jew and the Greek, for the same Lord over all is rich unto all that call upon Him. For whosoever shall call upon the Name of the Lord shall be saved."

This is a simple guarantee of salvation: "All men are equal in Christ. No matter how bad, or how good, if they repent, they become equal in the sight of God, at that time. Believing on Christ and calling upon Him is in effect the same thing, for did one not believe, he would no call upon Him."

Luke 18:10-13: the parable of the Pharisee and the Publican. The Pharisee said, "Look at me." The Publican said, "Don't look at me, please forgive me." The Pharisee was a hypocrite. The Publican was sincere.

John 3:16-17: "For God so loved the world, that He gave His only begotten Son, that whosoever believeth in Him, should not perish, but have everlasting life. For God sent not His Son into the world, to condemn the world, but that the world through Him might be saved." The next time the Son is sent to the world, it will be to judge.

Romans 8:38-39: "For I am persuaded, that neither death, nor life, nor angels, nor principalities, nor power, nor things present, nor things to come, nor height, nor depth, nor other creatures, shall be able to separate us from the love of God, which is in Christ Jesus, our Lord." Paul said, "I am persuaded that if we keep the teachings of Jesus and God's Word, there is nothing which can be able to separate our love from God, or God's love from us. One, who lives and walks in the spirit, will not be separated from God. The secret of Victory and absolute assurance, for the believer, is to walk, as taught by Paul, by the teachings of Jesus.

John 10:27-30: "My sheep, hear my voice, and I know them, and they follow Me. I give unto them, eternal life, and they shall never perish, neither shall any pluck them out of My hand. My Father, which gave them to me, is greater than all, and no man is able to pluck them out of My hand. I and My Father are One."

Three things, we must do and continue to do to receive eternal life:
1. "Believe": Which implies, complete and continued obedience.
2. "Hear His Voice:" Be not hearer only, but also be ye doers of His Word.
3. "Follow Christ." Not only at the beginning of a Christian experience, but daily and through out life. To claim eternal life, when one does not follow is like these Jews claiming to know God and have eternal life. Jesus declared, such, was not true.

The Father is greater than all the united forces of men, fallen angels, demons, and all enemies. No one, need fear of being snatched out of God's hand. The only thing, one must do, is come to God and permit His salvation and keeping power to be manifested. God cannot keep one contrary to His will any more than He kept Lucifer, Demons, Adam and Eve, and many others who chose to sin.

2 Cor 6:2: "For He saith, I have heard thee in a time accepted, and in the day of salvation, have I, succored thee, behold, now is the day of salvation."

Mark 16:16: "He that believeth and is baptized, shall be saved; but he that believeth not shall be damned. Two general results of preaching: 1) Saves the soul through faith or 2) Damns the soul through unbelief.

John 20:31: "But these are written that ye might believe that

Jesus is the Christ, the Son of God; and that believing ye might have life through His Name." Jesus says here: "I have written this to you, to prove beyond all doubt that Jesus of Nazareth is the promised Messiah and God's Son. That we might have full redemption and the benefits of the Gospel by faith."

Matthew 5:16: "Let your light so shine before men, that they may see your good works, and glorify your Father which is in Heaven." The purpose of all good works, among men, is to glorify the heavenly Father.

Many things glorify the Heavenly Father:
- For bodily healing.
- Christ's work of redemption.
- Answered prayer.
- Bearing much fruit.
- Helping God complete His work.
- See salvation of His creation.
- See miracles among men.
- Gifts ministered properly.
- Offering praise.
- Good works.
- Christian's Professions Many, many, more.

Luke 9:24-26: "For whosoever will save his life shall lose it; but whosoever will lose his life for My sake, the same shall save it. For what is a man advantaged, if he gain the whole world and lose himself, or be cast away? For whosoever shall be ashamed of Me and My Words, of Him shall the Son of man be ashamed, when He shall come in His own glory, and in His Father's, and of the holy angels."

In closing, I want to read, again to you, Romans10:9-13: "If thou shalt confess with thy mouth the Lord Jesus, and shall believe in thine heart that God hath raised Him from the dead, thou shalt be saved. For with the heart, man believeth unto righteousness, and with the mouth confession is made unto salvation. For the scripture saith, whosoever believeth on shall not be ashamed. For there is no difference between the Jew and the Greek, for the same Lord is over all and is rich unto all that calls upon Him. For whosoever shall call upon the Name of the Lord, shall be saved."

Amen?

Today Is Your Day of Salvation

Hear what God says, "Boast not thyself of tomorrow; for thou knowest not what a day may bring forth." Again, the Holy Ghost says, "Today if ye will hear His Voice, harden not your hearts." (Hebrews 3:7-8)

God is speaking today to you about, salvation through His Son, Jesus Christ. Yes today, for there may not be a tomorrow for you. It is important that you know, today, what God has to say about salvation, of your precious soul. Today God's love seeks you. God loves you. God's love seeks the soul of man. "For the Son of man is come to seek and to save that which is lost." (Luke 19:10)

God speaks to you, "Come now, and let us reason together, saith the Lord. Though your sins be as scarlet, they shall be as white as snow; though they be red like crimson, they shall be as wool." (Isa 1:18) God wants you unto Himself.

The cross of Calvary is God's eternal monument to the fact of His great Love for you. "He (Jesus) bearing His cross, went

106

forth into a place called the place of a skull, which is called in Hebrew, Golgotha, where they crucified Him, and two others with Him. One on either side, and Jesus, in their midst." (John 19:17-18) Now if you asked, "What does all of this mean?" To state it in a single sentence, He could say, "It means that God loves you, God wants you, and God seeks you." God is seeking you now with His powerful love.

We read in Revelation 3:20, "Behold, I stand at the door and knock; if any man hear My voice, and open the door, I will come in to him, and will sup with him, and he with Me."

Mary came to the Lord on behalf of her brother Lazarus. The Rich man came to Jesus on behalf of his son. The Mother came to Jesus on behalf of his servant, but Jesus came to the widow of Nain and raised her son from death unsolicited.

So Jesus comes to you today with powerful love that long has been seeking you out. Jesus has been bringing this to bear and that to bear on your life. Jesus has come to turn you toward Him. Maybe it was the death of your loved one, maybe you lost your job, or maybe through the message of the church. You have moved to think of your soul's salvation. Maybe the prayers of your godly mother or father have caught up with you. Jesus longs to love you. He longs to save you. He longs to share your loneliness, your sorrow, if you will let Him. He comes in love to you now. He is endeavoring to break down all your barriers to His love.

Some of us are fleeing God's Love right now. If you do not accept Jesus Christ as your Savior completely, if you do not know that your sins are forgiven, then you are fleeing God. If you die right now, will you go to Heaven? Some of you are fleeing because you fear that your temporary material possessions may be taken from you, that God will give you nothing in return.

There is a story, that I heard told about an incident that took place in the life of Gypsy Smith, the Evangelist (I forget where I read it; but it goes something like this): It is said, that a woman brought her son to the evangelist wanting him to shake hands with the man of God. The boy stretched forth his left hand. Mr. Smith requested the boy go give him the right hand, which was behind the boys back. The son refused to do so. Gypsy Smith, gently brought the boy's hand around to the front, and took his right hand, which was closed in a fist. The evangelist unclasped the fist and discovered the boy held a common clay marble in the palm of his hand. The boy would rather hold on to his clay marble than to shake hands with the man of God.

Isn't this a picture of man today? The spirit would introduce you to Jesus Christ, through His Word, but some of would hold back because they have in their life something they fear they would lose. They would rather hold on to their common clay marble, and refuse His precious diamond of salvation.

What does a man profit, if he shall gain the whole world, and lose his own soul? What shall a man give in exchange for his soul?" (Matt 16:26)

The love of God does not bring loss. It brings eternal gain. This eternal gain is free in Jesus Christ. "Come unto Me, all ye that labor and are heaven laden, and I will give you rest. Take My yoke upon you, and learn on me for I am meek and lonely in heart; and ye shall find rest unto your soul." This is the promise of Jesus Christ, Himself. (Matt 11:28)

"The blood of Jesus Christ His Son cleans us from all sin." (1 John 1:7)

In this life, "The Lord is my shepherd, I shall not want." (Psalm 23)

Are you fleeing from God on the path of pride? Why? When God calls you, should you be too proud to answer? Why should you feel that if you come to Jesus and bow down before Him and His love, why would you think you would be taking on a burden? God has been pursuing His children all through their life. He has been coming to you in Calvary's love. He is speaking to you now. He is speaking to you. This is the time given to you. It is no accident that you are hearing God's Word right now.

Where would you be, according to God's Word, if you died five hours ago? Yes, if you died five seconds ago? Would you end up in Hell or Heaven? You say I will accept Christ as my savior and Lord, tomorrow. You have no tomorrow. All the, tomorrows belong to God. All you have is today.

A great surgeon had just completed a serious operation. He then came to the loved ones and gave this report. "If the patient had come to me twelve years ago, I would have prescribed a medicine to prevent this. Yes, if he had come to me six years ago, I would have performed a minor operation; but I am afraid he came too late."

Every opportunity neglected is a tragedy. There is not one verse

109

in the Bible that backs you up in putting off salvation until tomorrow.

Neglected opportunity in your physical health can bring death.
Neglected opportunity in business can bring failure.
Neglected opportunity in study can cause a student to flunk.
Neglected opportunity in the care of your teeth will bring decay.
Neglected opportunity in salvation can end your soul in Hell.

As God's Word warns you against proposing what you will do tomorrow. "Where as you know not what shall be on the morrow. For what is your life? It is even a vapor, that appears for a little time and then vanishes away."

The devil knows your frame and inclinations. Therefore his trick is to get you to put off salvation in Christ. Don't let the devil trick you. The devil will try to make you believe you have another tomorrow to decide for Christ. This is a lie out of the pits of hell. God says, "Now." The devil says, "Tomorrow." The only time that you are sure of is now. You will not die in a tomorrow. You will die in a now. Now is the only assurance you have in this life. This very now, is being given to you, not by the devil, but by God. God controls all the now; therefore: "Now is the accepted time, behold, now is the day of salvation."(2 Cor 6:2)

Be assured that now if you accept Christ, "This day is salvation, come to this house." (Luke 19:9)

Remember: "For you have not got tomorrow, tomorrow will never arrive, though you plan and scheme. And you pray; and the timekeeper's hand hovers close to the bell. Mr. Man, Mrs.

Woman, Teenager, all you have, for sure, is today."

The Bible plainly warns, "Today, if you will hear His voice, harden not your hearts." (Heb 3:7-8)

But thank God you do have today. "Now is the accepted time; behold, now is the day of salvation." A day is something that has a beginning and an end. It is possible to wait too late to trust Christ as Savior.

There are two reasons why you should trust Christ now. First, you don't know when you will die. Death is uncertain. It calls at all hours and every age. When you die, it is too late then to trust Jesus Christ as Savior. Second, you don't know when Jesus may return. His coming has been predicted since New Testament times. He could come at any moment.

Matt 24:44 warns, "Be ye also ready, for in such an hour, as ye think not, the Son of man cometh."

Once Jesus comes, your destiny will be sealed. It will be too late, to trust Jesus Christ.

A Lesson From Paul
1 Corinthians 1:1-31

Paul, the Apostle to the Gentiles, called: "Saul."
A Benjamite, born in Tarsus, Asia Minor.
A Pharisee Educated at Jerusalem.
A Roman citizen, also a Jew.
He persecuted the Christian.
Converted to Christ, becoming a Preacher.

Paul wrote the letter to Corinth about 59 AD after some brethern from Corinth came and told him of some certain doctrines or teachings, and other problems of the church of Corinth.

What kind of a place was Corinth? In the time of the apostle, Corinth was the most important city of Greece. It was a city of culture, a commercial city, good for schools of philosophy and a city of wealth. It was also known for its wickedness and moral corruption. It worshipped Venus, and cults from Egypt and Asia. Also let us remember, one-half of the population consisted of slaves.

Paul was on his second great missionary journey, when he established the church at Corinth. Paul began his preaching in weakness and fear, and much trembling, but with a determination to be true to the Message of Christ and His cross. Paul had another vision from the Lord, to speak fearlessly and assured Paul of safety and success in his preaching.

Moved by envy, the Jews dragged the apostle before the judgment seat of Gallio. Gallio refused to hear the charges against Paul because Paul was a Roman citizen. Gallio, however, allowed the Greeks to beat Sosthenes, the ruler of the synagogue. Paul was permitted to preach the Gospel in Greece. The Roman government called this "religious tolerance."

On Paul's third missionary, during his long stay of three years in the city of Ephesus, he wrote this letter. (1 Corinthians)

Paul starts with a Salutation and a thanksgiving. Paul had been summoned to no common service. He designates himself as an "Apostle." Paul was an Apostle, an apostle by God's own appointment and will.

God has a plan, and it is known to Him from the beginning of the Ages. The Word of God, The Bible, is the revelation of that plan. God had a plan for Paul, now Paul knows this plan. God calls each one of us for something special, because each one of us is something special to God. Look at verse 2 of the first chapter of First Corinthians: "I write this to the Christian at Corinth, that are satisfied, in Christ Jesus. Also to those called to be saints, with all that is in every place, to those, that call upon the Name of Jesus Christ, our Lord, both theirs and ours."

So this is written to the church of Corinth, to them, that are sanctified in Christ. Sanctified means "To be separated from sin, and separated unto the services of God, to be pure and holy."

Paul is saying the church is a divine institution. God has established the Church. It belongs to God. It is the instrument of God. Man might speak foolishly about the church, but its origin is heavenly, its power will never be done away with. In the end it will be glorious.

The church had even been extended to the pagan city of Corinth. Out of this city of sin, morally corrupted, a brotherhood of believers had come into being.

Paul addresses this letter also to the brotherhood of saints. Not only those at Corinth, but unto "all that call upon the Name of our Lord Jesus Christ." Now their spirit was dividing them into contending groups, making them unmindful of other churches and disregarding of their practices and beliefs.

So thus, this letter is written for the church at Corinth, is intended for us. It is designed to give warning and guidance and inspiration to all members of all churches, until the end of the age.

Now look at verse 3 where Paul says, "Grace be unto you, and peace from God our Father, and the Lord Jesus Christ. Grace is a designation of the unmerited favor of God, and points to the source of all spiritual blessings. Peace is the resultant experience of the heart, which is opened by faith to receive all that God offers in and through Christ." So this is so far looking like a

114

prayer from Paul. It may well be our petition for one another and for ourselves.

Now in verses 4, 5, and 6, Paul follows by giving his thanks. Paul is grateful for the grace, which already has been shown to the Christians in Corinth, especially for the spiritual gifts by which they have become proud. As for the spiritual gifts by which they have been enriched gifts, it is true, of which they have become proud. Later on we will see Paul instructs the reader as to the value of these gifts and also administers a rebuke for their abuse. You are enriched by God in all Gifts, prophecy, utterances, the vocal gifts, and interpretations.

Paul enriches us in our teachings, doctrines of the Gospel, and the Testimony of Jesus Christ. We are enriched in everything, including all the gifts, and all the fruits of the spirit. Paul says, "Always render testimony." Paul says here to "always witness." It refers to the Gospel of Christ Jesus, which Paul had confirmed to men in all places by the gifts of the Holy Spirit.

Verse 7 is saying, while you are waiting on the coming of our Lord Jesus Christ, don't waste your time sitting around doing nothing, but go out and use the gifts the Holy Spirit has given you. Paul is saying that Christianity is a religion of action. The Old Testament says, "Why sit we here until we die?" Move Christian move.

So abundant was the grace thus granted that the Corinthian Christians lacked some of the spiritual gifts needed to sustain them in their life and work while they waited for the return of Christ. Paul says, in spite of trials and temptation, they will receive from the spirit of Christ, their needs and gifts needed for their life and work.

Trust not only in human nature, but trust also in the faithfulness of God, Who has called us into His fellowship with Christ. We should share also the anticipation of glory waiting for the revelation of our Lord Jesus Christ.

Verses 8 and 9: "That you may be blameless in the day of our Lord Jesus Christ. God is faithful. As the testimony, or Gospel, of Christ was confirmed among you to attract you to Christ, so He will confirm you through this testimony until the end, that you may be blameless at His coming."

Verse 10: "Speak the same thing; be perfectly joined together. Be in the same mind, same judgment. Remember Jesus prayed for the unity of believers. (John 17:11, 21-22) Be no divisions in the body of Christ. The members of this body should be perfected or fitted together, having the same intellectual convictions and opinions, and being thus united in faith and hope and love."

Verses 11 and 12: Now someone came and told Paul of contentions over human leadership, in the church of Corinth. These who came, protested that they submitted to no human teachers, but built their creed on the words of Christ Himself, all these claimed to be Christian, while more or severely opposing their fellow believes. Chloe was a very prominent person in Corinth, these contentions were caused by divisions of verse 10.

We find 4 main parties in Corinth:
1. **Paulians**: Followers of Paul, because he founded the church and because he was a special Apostle to the Gentiles.

116

2. **Apollonians**: Followers of Apollos, because of his eloquence.
3. **Cephins**: Followers of Peter, because he was the apostle to the Jews.
4. **Christians**: Followers of Christ, because they would have nothing to do with parties that followed men.

I think this is what we call denominations today. Each may confer some temporary benefit. It is the party spirit, expressed in rivalry and jealousy and bitterness and pride, which is to be deplored.

Paul says, "Apart from Christ there can be no real head for any body of believers." Was Paul crucified for you? No. If Christians remember who died for them, and to whom they therefore belong, they will be slow to say that they belong to Paul or Peter, Apollos or Cephas.

Were you baptized into the name of Paul? It was faith in Christ, not in any man, which they sealed and signified by baptism, and this faith brought them into a vital relation in Christ. Maybe that is why Paul said, "I thank God that I baptized none of you."

Paul goes on to say, "For Christ sent me not to baptize, but to preach the Gospel; not with wisdom or words, lest the cross of Christ should be made of none effect."

1. Paul was thankful that he had not emphasized or practiced baptism.
2. Christ sent him, not to baptize, but to preach the Gospel.
3. Baptism is not essential to salvation from sin. It is the symbol of the death burial and the resurrection of Jesus

Christ. (1 Peter 3:21)
4. Christ saves men before and without water baptism. (Verse 17-21)
5. The Gospel can be preached without the preacher being one to baptize.
6. The preaching of the cross, not baptism, is God's power to save.
7. Faith, not baptism saves the soul. It is important only after one is saved.

In verse 17 Paul writes that human eloquence is no substitute for the Holy Spirit anointing, power, and preaching. (Verse 17 and 2:1-5)

Christian ministers do now always realize that their supreme task is not that of administering finances of organizing churches, but of preaching the Gospel and they do not see that it may be possible to win for themselves followers who are not followers of Christ. They are not free from the peril of obscuring the great essential message of salvation by their very eloquence, and by their learned discussion of related themes.

Verses 18-25: Some say preaching of the cross is foolish, silly and absurd; but for us, who are being saved, salvation has a resent and future aspect.

The preaching of Christ, the Gospel, and the cross saves the souls of Mankind.

The One Talent Man
Matthew 25:14-30

It sometimes seems, as though, it is the small things that we overlook. Jesus told this parable for the benefit of the one talent person.

The parable tells of a man going on a trip to another country, put three of his servants in charge of some of his possessions. He gave one servant 5000 talents of his possessions, to another he gave 2000 talents, and to the last servant he gave 1000 talents. The man that received the 5000 talents invested it and soon doubled it. The man with the 2000 talents did likewise. He soon doubled his. Then we look at the man with the 1000 talents. This man had no faith in himself. He was afraid he would lose it and the master would be angry with him, so he buried it in the ground for safe keeping.

Soon the Master came home and the servant that he had been given the 5000 talents gave his master 10,000 talents, double of what the master had given him. The one that he had been given the 2000 shares had also doubled it. The master praised the two for their good works. Now the man that he had given the 1000 talents to said, "Master I knew you would deal with me harshly, that you are a strict man so I hid your 1000 talents in the ground, and here it is, all of it."

The talent or talents that were given to each of us vary. A talent is something one uses to achieve the purpose of the talent. It seems as though the ones with the one talent are liable to get discouraged and fearful. We often say, "What can I do with just one talent? Surly not too much is expected of me." You are wrong, just as much is expected from you. What is expected of you is your best. Sometimes too much is expected of one talent people, that is by people, not by God. Sometimes we think that we, with less talent, are not as important as the ones with more talents. That is not true. God expects our best, no matter how many talents we have. If the one talent man had doubled his to two talents, God would have praised him just as much as he did the ones with the five and two talents.

If I had sat here and said, "I am not going to teach or preach because I don't think I can do as well as John or Joe. I would feel inferior; I might try to copy their ways and their words instead of the ways and words that God puts upon my heart to say to each of you. I am not Billy Graham or Oral Roberts and I don't have their talents, but I do have a few talents and I use them as I feel God tells me to. When someone comes up to me and says, "Ed, if you had not taken time to teach me and talk to me about Jesus, I wouldn't be saved today." This has happened many times. I am not bragging. I just want you to know the one talent man can be just as important as the five talent man, more so if the five talent man doesn't do his best.

I think this parable is written for the person that says, "If I had a million dollars, I could go out and do it." Money has nothing to do with. We do not teach and preach for money, we teach and preach for God, because God told us too.

One talent people are tempted to take for granted is themselves. They fail to realize how much they are needed in this world. It is the One talent man that keeps "God's Church" going." It is the one talent man that holds "God's Church" together. I would rather have five people with one talent than one person with five talents. The five with only one talent, I believe, will out do the one with five talents.

If the one talented man had been true to his job, he would have entered into the joy of his Lord. I believe the more I do for God, the more God gives me to do. God will never give you more than the talents you have. The more I do, the more blessings I get, the more God does for me, and with me.

The real point of this message of Jesus is not that some have greater gifts than others, but that each one of us has his own contribution to make, large or small. We ought to discover this and put it to work. Every man's life is talented, with God given gifts. We are apart of God's plan. We then have a talent, we then have a gift, and God expects us to discover it and use it for His glory.

A talent is a present from God. God expects us to put it into circulation. We are a single thread in the total design of God's pattern. We are included in God's design. If we do not make our stitch in life, then something will be missing in His design. We may be only a one, talent servant, but we have the freedom to decide how we shall serve Him with that one talent. We can use it for God's glory or we can bury it, as a coward.

God will return and settle accounts with us, but who knows when? How have we been using our talents? Do we lock them up, some place where we can't get to them? Do we hide them like the one talent man in the parable, where they lay and rot away? Are going to use our talents only when we are forced to, or the least we can to get by with?

God expects an increase. God demands an increase. He holds us responsible for it. The quality of our devotion is tested within the tour of duty to which God assigns us, whether it be rich or poor or great or small. Greater gifts mean added responsibility. Much shall be required who has much. Each day's work is our way of saying, "Thank You God." We must do our work with our thoughts on God, for He is in charge. If we do this we find more and more is added to what we already have. Our gifts are multiplied in sharing, not diminished as is property and money when divided. Work done in loving service always brings rewards when we least expect. I have a file of letters and notes of all kind words, praise, thank you, Love notes from children, one thousand thanks, and best teacher. These things Money can't buy. These are some of my most precious possessions.

Of course there are a couple of dangers in life. The first is "envying those who seem to be more gifted," and second is, "pride in our own achievements. The best of us can claim to be no more than God's obedient and faithful servants." If we live up to God's expectations, we can expect to hear, "well done, thou good and faithful servant."

GRANDPA'S LESSONS ABOUT JESUS

The life we have is a great adventure doing God's work. Our work is a trust from God, a talent, of which God has invested in us. It is our duty to do all we can, with what He has given to us, and to have great joy in our work.

If you only have one talent, use it to God's glory and to satisfy God, or you will get just what God has promised you. That is the same thing He promised the one talent man that hid his one talent, and that outer darkness, crying and gnashing of teeth in eternity. God called him "wicked" and "lazy."

Jesus, who is "one with the Father", exhibited the quality of obedience. So this text reminds us that we are not in the business of Christian living alone. We are in it with God. This relationship is possible only, if we are obedient to God's demands.

God doesn't want anybody around that doesn't obey Him. How happy we will be when we stand before Jesus and hear Him say to us. "Thank you, well done, My good and faithful servant." Amen?

Come See A Man Called Jesus

John 4:29: The Samaritan woman ran all over town and shouted, "Come see a man." She didn't say, come see a church. She did not say come see an organization. She did not preach education, talents, or rituals. She preached Jesus Christ. Although she did not hold papers, she preached Jesus and won a whole city to God.

When Philip met the treasurer of Ethiopia, a eunuch of great authority, under Candace the Queen of Ethiopia. This eunuch was reading from the book of Isaiah. The Holy Spirit told Philip, "Go over and walk along beside the chariot." Philip ran over and said, "Do you understand what you are reading?" The eunuch replied, "of course not, how can I when there is no one to instruct me?" He asked Philip to come up into the chariot and talk to him. Right then and there, Philip opened his mouth and preached unto him Jesus, philosophy would not do it. But there is power in the Name of Jesus. That man took Jesus back to his people and the result was that the whole continent received the Gospel of the Lord Jesus Christ. All this because Philip opened his mouth and preached to him Jesus. (Acts 8:35)

GRANDPA'S LESSONS ABOUT JESUS

Peter looked into the faces of that mob of Jews and told them about Jesus. When Paul was brought before governors, Kings, and Rulers, he arose and explained to them that Jesus was the theme of the time. Educated Paul determined to know nothing except Jesus Christ and Him crucified, for Christ is the spirit of the Gospel, which is the power of God unto salvation to all people. We need the power of the wonderful Christ to rest upon us.

In the book of Isaiah 9:6: "For unto us a Child is born, unto us a Son is given, and the government shall be upon His shoulders, and His Name shall be wonderful, counselor, the mighty God, the everlasting Father, the Prince of Peace." I looked up the word wonderful, and it means, "marvelous, extra ordinary, exciting, and magnificent." Every time I write the word wonderful, I want to remember these words. Every time you hear this word wonderful, I want you to remember these words, marvelous, extra ordinary, exciting, and magnificent. This is, in part, a description of the wonder of Jesus.

It seems to me that Isaiah was a "Gospel Preacher" of the Old Testament. He preached as much Gospel as any of the writers in the New Testament. He saw Jesus as He was, high and lifted up. Isaiah was never the same again. He got out from the church that had people with unclean lips and got into a church with the people who had had a coal of fire touched to their tongues, which said, "Here am I, Lord, send Me." Isaiah seemed to look far ahead, down through time into the future, and saw Jesus as He hung on the cross, and said, "and with His stripes we are healed." He received his healing through the atonement, in the same way we can today. He saw King Hezekiah healed after he told the king about God. They knew where the healing came from. Isaiah did not take the glory, but gave it all to God.

Isaiah knew about the wonderful Christ through the Holy Spirit. Through the Holy Spirit, Isaiah wrote: "And the spirit of the Lord shall be upon Him, the spirit of wisdom and understanding, the spirit of counsel, and might, the spirit of knowledge, and of fear of the Lord." (Isaiah 11:2)

People have and will seek for years to be saved from Hell. They are thinking of themselves. They want to be saved, just to keep from going to torment. If they would seek the savior instead of seeking to be saved, they would receive something. Get in love with the Savior; get the wonderful Christ into your life. The things of the world will then fade away and with Jesus you will never be the same. You will be Christ like.

If you are seeking to be saved, seek a person. When I was married, I did not receive a "marriage religion" I did not get theology. I did not join something or become a member of anything. I received a person. When I was saved I did not get religion, which I already had, but I received a Savior. I became acquainted with a person, a friend, and companion. Jesus became a part of me.

People will try for years to be delivered from bad habits, just because their church does not believe in bad habits. They want to be like other members. They want to be popular with their church. They want to measure up to the standards required by people. Some know that the habits are not good for them, so they want better health. All this is wonderful, but wouldn't it be better and easier, if they would seek Jesus until they became so full of the divine nature and virtue of Christ that the habits would no longer stay there? Would it not be a better motive to want to become like Jesus Christ?

Jesus said, "When the Holy Spirit comes, He will not speak of himself, but He will take Jesus and show Him unto you. He will speak of Jesus." (John 16:13)

When we preach about receiving the Holy Spirit, many people will say, "I think you should exalt Christ instead of the Holy Spirit." My friends, the Holy Spirit will make Jesus a hundred times more real in your life. "He shall glorify Me," said Jesus. (John 16:13)

Many people will seek healing, just in order to be healed, so that they will not suffer, or so they will not need to spend money for a doctor. If they would get in love with the Healer, they would receive the divine nature and all things that pertain to life and Godliness.

Some people would like to steal healing, without confession that they are in love with the healer. They want healing, but they do not want the healer. They would go to a witch doctor just as quickly or a littler quicker. They would go to a spirit medium, because the spiritualists do not require one to stop committing their sins. They can still lie, cheat and steal and yet receive treatments.

Jesus treats all people alike. All classes of people look the same to Jesus, regardless of their race, creed, or color. Jesus demands obedience. Jesus required people to obey Him in Bible times. He is just the same yesterday, today and forever. Far too many people do not know how to seek the gifts Jesus has to offer. If they would seek the giver, and then the gifts would take care of them selves. Jesus can be in your life, doing the same work He once did. He can dwell within.

I know One that can lay hands on you and you will never be the same again. It will pay you to go any distance to get this One to lay hands on you. His name is Jesus. I said His name is Jesus. All this is right. Instead of seeking the gifts, we need to get in love with the giver, become more like Him. He is our example.

In all my Bible studies, I have never read that people went around bragging that they had so many gifts, but did not know how to use them. I read that Peter, instead of trying to figure out what he had, telling the name and the number of gifts, Peter said, "Such as I have give I thee, and it worked! The man, who had been lame from his mother's womb, jumped up and walked." (Acts 3:1-7)

Peter had also made a discovery that it was not his power or holiness; but it was the Name of Jesus. I wish we could make the same discovery. "Ye men of Israel, why marvel ye at this? Why look ye so earnestly on us, as though by our own power or holiness we had made this man to walk? In His name, through faith in His name hath made this man strong, whom ye see and know; yea, the faith, which is by Him, hath given him this perfect soundness in the presence of you all." (Acts 3:12-16)

When I can testify about Jesus and make people want Him, then I will have made a success as a minister.

Philip went down to Samaria and preached Christ unto them. (Acts 8:5). Unclean spirits came out crying with loud voices.

Both men and women were saved and baptized. We need more men who will go down to another class of people and preach Jesus unto them.

Peter went to the household of Cornelius, and opened his mouth and preached them Jesus. (Acts 10:38). While he was yet preaching the Holy Spirit fell upon all them that heard the Word.

Paul said, "For we preach not ourselves, but Christ Jesus the Lord; and all that we say about ourselves, is that we are His servants; because of what Jesus has done for us." (2 Cor 4:5)

Peter was on the mountaintop. He had a wonderful experience, but his trouble was, he wanted to remain on that one mountaintop. People today are yet trying to build a tabernacle to Elijah. They carry a chart and preach prophecy. They tell you how wonderful Jesus will be during the thousand-year reign and how the devil will be bound and over thrown, but Jesus is wonderful now. The devil can be bound and over thrown in your life now.

The Pharisees had prophecy figured out a certain way. They had the first coming of Jesus. They had Him coming in a certain way and at a certain time. They had their minds and thoughts upon how and when and where Jesus would come that they missed Jesus when He did come. They loved the doctrine about Jesus more than they did Jesus himself. It is possible to have Pharisees today. They may spend much of their time, figuring out the time, of the second coming of Jesus, and neglect Jesus. They may miss His second coming, especially if they hate all other groups of Christians.

GRANDPA'S LESSONS ABOUT JESUS

"Do you want to go to Heaven, just so you will not go to hell, or do you want to go to Heaven to be with Jesus? If you want to go to Heaven, to be with Jesus, then why don't you want to be with Jesus now?" We call Him Lord, Lord, but we do not do the things that He says. We put His name on our churches. We use His Name in praying in ceremonies and rituals. But then we condemn everyone else to hell that does not say the same ceremony or ritual exactly as we say it. We have many churches today that want to put Jesus' Name on their church, but they do not want His garments, theories and pet doctrines. They want to find fault with things of the church that doesn't amount to a hill of beans. They want to build their self, a name in the church instead of Jesus Name.

On the Mount of Transfiguration, God spoke and said, "This is My beloved Son, hear ye Him." That is what He is saying to us today. That is what we all should do. We should hear the Lord for ourselves instead of being to and fro with every wind of doctrine.

The woman at the well said, "Come and see a Man that told me all things I ever did." She did not say, "Come see a church." She did not say. "Come see an organization." She did not say, "Come and see me." She preached Jesus. "Come see a man that told me all ever I did."

Some day you will stand before Jesus. At that time you will either confess all you did or He will tell you. You will stand before Jesus.

I don't care if I teach you anything else about the time that Christ will come again, because I do not know the time. All I want to tell you is this: "Listen to me, come, let me show you a man. A man, if you come to know Jesus, you won't worry about the second coming. You will be prepared."

Jesus knew this woman's sins. She confessed. Jesus Forgave. Jesus forgot her sins.

You won't worry about the end of the world. You won't worry about dying. Come let us learn together about a man that can tell you all that ever you did. Come and let Him tell you all that you can do, if you will but listen to him. Drink of this Living Water (The Holy Spirit) that you will never thirst again.

Come See A Man Called Jesus, and you will never be the same again.

There Is A Way

All things are possible through faith and prayer (Matt 15:21-28)
But only if you believe. There is a way.

I wish I could say one thing until you would hear it in your heart
as well as see it with your eyes and hear it with your ears. "There
is a way." If that ever sinks into the depth of your heart, you will
be a new person. There is a way for every good thing. There is a
way to accomplish everything you should accomplish. If you are
seeking healing, there is a way to receive it. If you are seeking
salvation, there is a way to receive it. Whatever you need, the
answer has already been prepared. There is definitely a way to
God.

There are certain things I cannot understand. On the other hand,
I find as I believe in the Bible, these things are made plain and
clear. I cannot see them through myself or in my own mind; but
I can see them through Christ's Mind, through Christ's Power.
There is a way. There is a way because the scriptures say, "All
things are possible to them that believe." Remember we still
have our freedom of choice, whether it be physical, spiritual,

132

mental, social, or worldly.

Most people I meet want help from God. Many times their only hope is through God's Power. However, many of them, when they are rebuffed or hindered, throw up their hands with a negative attitude and surrender themselves to their present predicament. They are not aware of this great truth. There is a way. There is an answer to their problems.

The very first condition of faith and its fulfillment is to believe that there is a God that God exists. Hebrews 11:6 states, "He that comes to God must believe that He is, and that He rewards them, that diligently seek Him."

The next condition of faith and its fulfillment is to believe that God cares. God is great. God is good. He wants to reward those who diligently seek Him and believes in Him. How God comes to us in some unexplainable, and some mysterious way and at exactly the right moment is something we may never understand. But the important thing is that God comes through good times, through our bad times, and through our troubles and always at the exact time to our side to help us.

Now I want to tell you about a woman who discovered the formula. I think one of the most moving stories in the Bible is in Matthew 15. It is about a mother whose child was insane. This woman was not an Israelite. She was not a follower of Jesus. She was a Canaanite, a member of a vicious, unclean tribe of people. What she did is important to people of all generations and especially to us today. When all else had failed, she said within herself, I know there is a way, and if I can find it and get to Christ or His followers, my child will be healed. So she came

133

fearfully to the disciples and said to them, "Sirs, my daughter is afflicted with insanity. Will you pray for her?" They turned and walked away. But they couldn't get away from her. She kept following, saying, "Men of God, please, pray for my child." Finally they stopped, and requested that Jesus dismiss her. She is crying after us." Then Christ Himself rebuffed the woman and then talking to His disciples, answered, "I am not sent, except to the sheep who have strayed away from Israel."

By that Jesus meant people like this woman have no right to be here. She has never followed God. The Israelites have followed God for centuries. Some of them have strayed away, but there is hope through me to get them back. I came down here to seek and to save them. But there isn't much hope for a person like this, and then Jesus moved away. Jesus had always planned to offer salvation to the gentiles. First He had to offer salvation to the Jew, for they were God's chosen people.

The Bible says, she came up to Him again and worshipped Him. That took a great deal of humility and determination. Then unwittingly she used an infallible formula. She said, "Lord help me." That is a strange thing for Jesus to refuse. "Lord, help me." Now for the first time Jesus recognized her presence. "Woman," Jesus said, "It is not right to take the children's bread and give it to the dogs." That sounds like that was pretty rough treatment. She was being ignored by Christ. She was pushed aside by the disciples. Now she was counted as not having any rights at all by Jesus. Now she was called a dog.

To appreciate Christ's stand here, you must realize that the children of Israel were the chosen people. They were chosen because they believed in, Jehovah God. God didn't just pick them out and say, "I love them above all the rest." Abraham in centuries past found in his heart a love for God. Abraham passed it to his son Isaac, and Isaac to his son. Jacob, and Jacob to his twelve sons, and the twelve sons to their offspring. On to the twelve tribes of Israel until a great nation was built. And the children of Israel, even though they were not perfect, were the only nation in the world who worshipped the true God.

When Christ came, many of these had strayed away, but the gentile world had never paid any attention to God. The Romans had conquered the world. They were even the overlords of the children of Israel at that time. What did the gentiles care about God? They were vicious and wild, dog like, in their nature. They were against every thing and snapping their teeth at their fellow man. So the word dog was used loosely to describe the gentile world two thousand years ago.

Now one of them needed healing for her child. Jesus was going to teach her a lesson, and if she was like all the rest that was all she wanted. She wasn't concerned about serving God or believing in Him. She came for only one purpose, to get Jesus to heal her child. Do this and I will leave you alone, she was thinking. She simply wanted something for her child and if she got that, then God wouldn't matter any more. She would go from there and do as she pleased. That was what Christ faced in dealing with this woman. Some people are like that today.

Now Jesus had to answer her in these ways. Jesus had to challenge her request in what was apparently a cruel manner. It was not that He did not love her. He did this to see if she really believed, if she was sincere. He did this to let the woman do some thinking about her self. Sometimes God and His servants give us a certain treatment that is hard to explain. If you are easily offended, you probably will be offended rather quickly, because Christ is concerned about your soul as well as your body. He is concerned about how you live. How you believe. How you worship. This was also His concern for the woman.

The Woman would not take no for an answer. This woman made a heroic effort. She refused to be pushed off. She would not take no for an answer. She still believed. There is a way she thought. Can you realize what this means? How many of us here have failed to receive the help you needed and wanted so desperately? Have you tried once or twice, then given up? Have you accepted defeat? Or do you still firmly believe there is a way?

In order to get help, this woman was willing to surrender her pride. When Jesus said, "It's not right to take the children's bread and give it to dogs." She said, "Yes, Lord, that's right." She admitted the kind of person she was. "I have not lived the kind of life that is right." Now that took a great amount of courage, but she appealed to His love. She knew that justice would deny her the right to petition Him, because she was a sinful woman. So she humbly reminded Him, "Even so Lord, every man in Israel, who has a little house dog, let his children take the crumbs from their table and give it to the little dog… Now, you have just said that it is not right to take the children's bread and give it to the dogs. That is true. The little dog is not worth that much. The master of Israel allows his children to take their scraps and crumbs and give then to the little dog so it can live and not die. Lord, I know you love my little girl as much as that man loves that little dog. I know you will give me a crumb so my little girl can live."

136

Talk about buttering up to the Lord, this is it. She knew Jesus loved people. Jesus loved sick children, He loved people who were unfortunate and in trouble and in need. She had heard about Jesus and what He had done all over Israel, how He had cast out demons and healed sick people and raised up little children. She knew all this. She believed it and that is how she built up her faith. What she was saying is this: "Lord the reason this man lets his children take their scraps, and give them to the little dog is so it can live. It is because you put love in his heart, and if you put love in a man's heart for his little dog, I know you have love in your own heart to heal my sick child." Oh, what a way to approach God.

You, who are in need of healing, have you ever approached God like this? Have you ever said to Him, "God, if you let a flower bloom on a rocky hillside where there is very little moisture, won't you let me bloom in health and strength and salvation? If you feed a little, worthless sparrow, won't you put bread on my table? If you clothe the flowers in the garden and lilies of the field, won't you give us clothes to wear?"

This is the right approach. Why didn't you appeal to God's love? Why not come to Him in the way that pleases Him most? The Bible says, "God is love." We forget that and judge God by people. That is wrong, but the Bible says, "God is not a man." God is too good to do wrong, too wise to make a mistake and too strong to fail.

This woman in everything she did said, "There is a way. There is a way for my child to be healed of God." She knew that only a crumb from His table was more than enough to meet her need.

The woman got what she asked for. Then the Lord said to her, "Woman, great is thy faith. Be it unto thee even as thou wilt." Or in modern words, "even as you will." She put her will into her faith. There is something in the human being called "will," that rises up in emergencies and gives the Human being the extra power to help us meet emergencies, just floods our beings in spiritual things. We call it our "will." This "will," to accomplish the impossible, can be used in a spiritual way, also. Have you ever turned that power called "will" toward God? This woman did. Normally, she would not have had the courage to go through all that she did, to be sent away from the disciples, rebuffed by Jesus, called a dog and to be insulted. But that "will" rose up in her. There is a way. There is a way for my child to be healed. What does it matter if I am insulted? My child is lying there insane, and Christ has the power to make her whole. I'll go through anything; I'll take any insult if it can bring healing to my child. And "will" in her came surging out of her heart, and made her faith, great faith. Jesus saw that and said, "It will be exactly what you "will" it to be." Her daughter was healed.

I believe that faith is part of "will." To try to have faith without "will" power, is to have half-faith, or little faith. There must be that determination, that character that stands up and dares to believe God, that knows, that God wants us to have His blessings and will settle for nothing less.

I believe it is God's will to heal. Christ came to take our infirmities and bear our sicknesses. Matthew 8:16-17 states: "When the evening had come, they brought unto Him a man that was possessed with devils. And He cast out the spirits, with His Word, and healed all that were sick, that it might be fulfilled which was spoken by Isaiah the prophet, saying, Himself took our infirmities, and bare our sickness."

I believe that there is a way to God. In my opinion no one has the right to write over his body or his soul, "No Hope." Rather, he should write, "There is a way, there is a way to receive help from the Lord."

God may choose to heal you through medical skill or some other medium. There is healing to be found through climate, through love and understanding and through prayer. God may choose one, or two, or all of these methods. He may choose to heal you solely by prayer, but I believe there is a way.

We must use our "will" Power, our faith in Him. Our faith must declare without reservation or fear, "There is a way, and I will find that way, to God." We hold the keys to our faith and healing. We hold the key to answered prayer. The price has already been paid. Jesus paid it on Calvary. You must know there is a way to God. Then, move on and on to claim it. It belongs to you.

There is a way. And the way is through Jesus Christ.

Are Your Prayers Answered?

Hear the Words of Jesus, as He tells this parable to His disciples.

Luke 18:1-7: One day Jesus told His disciples a story to illustrate their need for constant prayer and to show them that they must keep praying until the answer comes. There was a city judge, a very godless man, who had great contempt for everyone. A widow of that city came to him frequently to appeal for justice against a man who had harmed her. The judge ignored her for a while, but soon she got on his nerves. I fear neither God nor man, the judge said to himself, but this woman bothers me. I'm going to see that she gets justice, for she is wearing me out with her constant coming. Then the Lord said, "If even an evil judge can be worn down like that, don't you think that God will surely give justice to His people who plead with Him day and night?"

This parable illustrates the necessity of persevering when prayer is not answered immediately. This widow came repeatedly, pestering the judge beyond endurance, which was the secret of her success in getting an answer to her request. The pestering went on without a let up, and changed the picture. After the judge tolerated her pestering to the breaking point, he concluded that he would never have any more peace until he got rid of her and the only way to do this was by granting her request, which she was right according to law. The pestering went on without letting up, and changed the picture.

Because of the mental pressure the judge said, "She has put me to the point of exhaustion, by her perpetual coming, she harasses or pesters me beyond my endurance." No wonder the big, hardhearted judge became willing to see that she got justice.

In verse 6, Jesus says, "Hear what the unjust judge saith." This is the point of the parable, if such methods as the widow used would get results from an infidel of utter selfishness and unconcern for the needs and rights of others, how much more can children of God get results in prayer by the same methods.

Remember what the widow asked for now? Not something just to be asking or testing the judge; but she asked for what the Word of the law promised her, Justice.

We too can expect only what the word of God has promised us in answer to prayer. A judge of injustice becomes a judge of justice through a little woman using the proper means.

Verse 7: "And shall not God avenge His own elect, which cry day and night unto Him, though he bear long with them? I tell you that He will avenge them speedily. Nevertheless when the Son of man cometh, shall He find faith on the earth?"

This is Christ's assurance that prayer will be answered. Now we found that the widow woman used the proper plan and means.

141

What are the proper means for prayer, answered prayer, for God's people? Let us go back to Matthew 7:7-8: "Ask, and it shall be given you; seek, and ye shall find; knock, and it shall be opened unto you. For every one that asketh, receiveth; and he that seeketh fineth; and to him that knocketh it shall be opened."

The idea here is to demand something that is due one because of family and redemptive rights. Five times it is found in verse 7-11. The first letters of ask, seek, and knock, spells ask. It is God's will that we ask and get what we want.

Seeking must be with the whole heart. Get what is due us through His Word. The way of getting an answer to prayer is to ask which implies want; seeking, which implies loss; and knocking, which implies need. One must ask with confidence and humility; seek with care and application; knock with earnestness and perseverance. It reads, for everyone that asketh, receiveth; and he that seeketh, findeth and to him that knocketh, it shall be opened. All these things must be done in accordance to His Word. You must be a believer.

There is no exception to the rule for anyone. If there is, it is because of the failure to ask in faith, nothing wavering. James writes in the book of James 1:5-8, "If any of you lack wisdom, let him ask of God, that giveth to all men liberally, and faithfully; and it shall be given unto him. But let him ask in faith, nothing wavering. For he that wavereth is like a wave of the sea driven by the wind and tossed to and fro. For let not, that man think that he shall receiveth any thing of the Lord. A double, minded man is unstable in all his ways."

He who doubts is like a wave that is rising one moment and

sinking the next. One minute he believes and another he does not. He says yes, and then no, to what God has promised, never making up his mind what he believes. He staggers helpless in prayer like a drunken man. It is certain that a doubtful man will not get an answer. Double minded is a Jewish term used to describe a man who attempted to worship God and still loved the creature; who wished to secure both worlds. He would not give up the world here and yet was not going to give up heaven. One torn between carnal and spiritual things is a double-minded man.

Unbelief is caused by wrong teachings. The promises are unlimited. So if there is a limitation in answer, there is a limitation of faith, not of God's will or power. The door is never opened in the East until the one who knocks is first questioned. Note the three-fold assurance of an answer, receiveth, findeth, it shall be opened.

Romans 4:20-25 Paul writes: "Abraham staggered, not at the promise of God through unbelief; but was strong in faith, giving glory to God; and being fully persuaded, that what he had promised, he was able also to perform. Therefore it was imputed to him for righteousness. Now it was not written for his sake alone, that it was imputed to him. But for us also, to whom it shall be imputed, if we believe on Him that raised up Jesus our Lord, from the dead; who was delivered, for our offenses and was raised again for our justification. Abraham's soul was full of confidence that the Word of God bound him do fulfill what he had promised. The Word and Promises was written for all men. The condition of the Gospel is faith, not only temporary faith, but steadfast and continued faith. Jesus died for our sins and was resurrected for our justification. Let us remember this."

Luke 11:22-26 "Jesus said unto them, 'Have faith in God. For verily, I say unto you, that whosoever shall say unto this mountain, be thou removed, and be thou cast into the sea, and shall not doubt in his heart; but shall believe that those things. Whatsoever he saith, shall come to pass, he shall have what so ever he saith. Therefore I say unto you, what things so ever ye desire, when ye pray, believe that ye receive them, and ye shall have them.'" (Jesus said this.)

But Jesus goes on to say, "And when ye stand praying, forgive, If ye have ought against any, that your father also which is in heaven may forgive you your trespasses. But if ye do not forgive, neither will your father which is in heaven forgive your trespasses."

Such is possible or it would not be a command. Man was created with God's faith, but doubt entered in at the fall. Faith is restored in the new birth and if normally exercised and maintained it will grow to fullness and power.

Verses 23-24 are considered merely as promises, but they can also be considered as conditional prophecy to be fulfilled when certain terms are met. Here, faith without doubting is the condition to meet if one wants the fulfillment of the benefits. The prediction or promise is that everyone who meets the condition will be answered, even to the moving of a mountain. (A mountain is, or can be, anything that stands between you and God.) Do you have a mountain in your life that needs removed?

Jesus says in Matthew 18:19-20, "Again I say unto you, that if two of you shall agree on earth as touching anything, that they shall ask, it will be done for them of My Father which is in

144

heaven. For where two or three are gathered together in My Name, there am I in the midst of them." Two can move God to get whatever they ask, and agree upon in prayer; but two can constitute a local church with God's presence assured in Christ. Christ is among all believers.

When Jesus says, "In My Name," Jesus is saying, "In My Way, according to My Word." Have faith in God, Faith believing, no doubting. Have faith believing in Jesus' Name.

The Spirit Filled Life

Some years ago the Lord searched my heart on this subject of the Holy Spirit and His ministry. I asked myself some questions. I wonder if the people of God's Church really know about the Holy Spirit? I have tried to preach and teach to you the Word of God. One person said to me, "It looks to me like God's Church is going to become like a Pentecostal Church." I said in my heart, "I sure hope it does! I would give anything if it would get more like the church at Pentecost, in Biblical times."

We should not let people who are in error take away from us the blessed teaching of the power of the Holy Spirit. Go to the Bible and see what it says and whatsoever it says, ask God to give, just that, nothing less, nothing more.

There is an absence of emphasis upon the Holy Spirit of God. One day when John the Baptist was preaching, he said, "There stands one among you who you know not." Talking about Jesus Christ and I wonder if that couldn't be said of people and churches today? "There stands one among you who you know not, the Holy Spirit of God"?

146

In Acts 19:2: When Paul went to Ephesus, and saw these Ephesian believers, he said, "Have you received the Holy Spirit, since you believed?" They said unto him, "We have not so much as heard whether there be any Holy Spirit." There is a tremendous lack of emphasis and preaching on the Holy Spirit and His work in the life of God's children today.

The Holy Spirit resides, but He does not always preside. The Holy Spirit should be in every believer. You need never to ask God to give you the Holy Spirit, because you already have the Holy Spirit available. "What, know ye not, your body is the temple of the Holy Spirit, which is in you, which ye have of God, and ye are not your own? For ye are bought with a price." He resides always in the heart and life of every Christian; but He does not always preside."

The Holy Spirit presided in the Church at Antioch when men prayed and were led and directed of the Holy Spirit. "If any man have not the Spirit of Christ; he is none of His." He always indwells. We always have Him, but He does not always have all of us. "As many as are led by the Spirit of God, they are the sons of God."

A lady once said to a wise preacher, "I want to tell you something wonderful that happened to me. Last night I received the Holy Ghost." This preacher said something that startled the lady. He said, "I know something even better than that. Now let the Holy Spirit get all of you, then you will have it all." Yes, we do always have Him, but He does not always have us.

Peter and John were sent to where Philip was preaching and things happened. People were saved, miracles were wrought, and the sick were made well. The power of God was there. Even Simon the sorcerer said, "Give me also this power." Offering Peter money. He was rebuked by Peter who said, "Thy money perish with thee." We need to ask God for this power, not try and buy it.

I want to ask you what would your answer be if some inquiring soul asked you this morning, "Are you filled with the Holy Spirit?" God's wonderful Word says to every believer, "Be ye filled with the Holy Spirit." John the Baptist was filled with the Spirit of God. In Luke 1:15, we read here an angel from God said to his praying father and mother about the coming baby. He said, "He shall be great in the sight of the Lord, and shall drink neither wine nor strong drink, and he shall be filled with the Holy Spirit, even from his mother womb." (They are talking about John the Baptist.)

See our blessed Lord walk out in the river Jordan where John was baptizing and say, "John, baptize me now." When John was reluctant to do so Jesus said, "Go ahead, baptize me, for thus it becomes us to fulfill all righteousness."

Jesus had a body like yours and mine. He knew what it was to live in the flesh. That was what the incarnation was, deity dwelling in a human body. John the Baptist put his hands on that human body, buried Him in the waters of baptism and brought Him up again. The heavens opened and God, with an audible voice, said, "This is My beloved Son, in whom I am well pleased."

A man visiting Niagara Falls said, as he looked upon the great falls, "This is probably the greatest power in the world." The

148

reply from a minister friend said, "No, my brother, the greatest power in the world is a Christian filled with the Holy Spirit."

I think the greatest advice any one ever gave me was, "Ed, don't preach beyond your experience. You can't put a 50-year-old mind in a 5-year-old preacher... Don't preach about anything that you don't know anything about. Don't preach about something that you haven't experienced yourself. Don't preach beyond your experience."

The Bible says that if you are to be filled with the Spirit of God, you must have a desire. You must want to be filled and be afraid of being filled. You must forget about the cost. You must have a hunger and thirst. You must want to be filled with the Holy Spirit of God. I am not just talking about preachers, but to every Christian. Every Christian lady ought to be filled with the Spirit of God, as should every father, mother, Sunday school teacher, song leader and every musician. "Be ye filled with the Holy Spirit."

My friends, it matters not what programs we have, what organizations we have. If we do not have the Power of God in our lives, our work will burn at the judgment seat, like wood, hay and stubble. To be thirsty and hungry, for the filling of Holy Spirit is born in us.

Now the Bible says and common sense tells us that before you fill something, this something must be empty. Easily said, but difficult to do. If, you are to be filled, you must be emptied. "Be ye not drunk with wine where in is excess." Do not have something else contrary to the Holy Spirit." God won't fill a dirty vessel. God won't pour His Holy Spirit in all of His fullness into somebody's vessel that already has something in it contrary to the will of God. God only fills empty vessels. God says, "Oh, if only My people could come up to My house with an empty cup and hold it up and cry from a thirsty soul, "O God, fill my cup to overflowing."

Sister, I can't put good, clean, white milk in a pitcher that already has something in it. Wash it and come back and I will fill it up.

I think, maybe, God is saying to us in the crucial hour, "Empty the pitcher, and clean it out, get ready, then I will fill it." If we would be filled, we must be thirsty. If we would be filled, we must be empty. If we would be filled, we must be obedient. "As many as are led by the Spirit of God." For God to give us His power, we must obey Him.

If you would be filled with the Holy Spirit, you need to ask God to fill you. When the day of Pentecost came, they not only were anointed, they were filled with the Holy Spirit. They prayed. In Acts 4:31, the Bible says, "And when they had prayed. The place was shaken where they were assembled together, and they were all filled with the Holy Ghost." The Holy Spirit of God will fill us so we can exalt the Lord. "He shall not speak of Himself, He shall glorify Me." If you want the fullness of the Holy Spirit, it will only be when you are willing to let the Spirit glorify Jesus in your life.

You will have powerful witnessing. I like what I read in the Bible. Yes, they put Paul and Silas in Jail and beat them, and misused them, and looked lightly upon them. No doubt, laughed at them. But at midnight an earthquake came and the jail was destroyed and whole families got saved and baptized, all because they had the power to witness. Yes they were thrown in jail in the fourth chapter of the book of Acts, but a lame man got healed in chapter three. They took him by the hand and Peter said, "Silver and gold have I not, but such as I have give I thee. In the Name of Jesus of Nazareth, rise up and walk. The lame man stood, leaping and praising God." I think this lame man stuck so close to them that he also, was in jail with them that night.

Why do we not win souls? We don't have the power of God. We don't have the fullness of the Holy Spirit. The fullness of the Holy Spirit is given to overcome difficulty.

Oh, how often we preach on Zechariah 4:5-7, where it says that, the Spirit of the Lord, the power of God, a double portion of God's Spirit etc. All are talking about the power of the Spirit of God. Zechariah is writing to people of God having to build the walls around Jerusalem. There were many enemies. They were being laughed at and fought against. People united against them. And Zechariah wrote about it, "Not by might, nor by power, but by the Spirit, saith the Lord." Then the scriptures cry, "O! Mountain this mountain is of difficulty, thou shalt be made a plain." God said, "I will level your mountains when you are filled with the Holy Spirit of God."

My people today we are like Elijah under the Juniper tree, all alone. Maybe like Elijah, and you are saying, "I might as well die and get it over with." You know the answer to that? The fullness of the Holy Spirit is the answer. He gives us power to overcome and the ability to bear fruit.

Who is thinking about the fruits of the Spirit today? They are love, joy, peace, goodness, meekness, kindness, temperance and faith? Who wants to love one another?

Suppose at the day of Pentecost (all of the disciples were there, but only one was preaching), old John had said, "Now, you know, I don't understand all this. Peter is an unlettered man, and so am I." Peter was a fisherman, and one day the Lord came along and Andrew brought him and got saved. One day Jesus came along and said. "Put down your nets and follow me." And Peter never went to college. He hadn't been to seminary. He is always opening his mouth and putting his foot in it, always speaking without thinking. Suppose John had said on that day of Pentecost, "Why didn't the Lord have me up there preaching?"

Suppose James had said, "I am probably looked upon as the leader of the church. It seems I ought to have been up there preaching if Pentecost is going to come." Listen, if James and John and Thomas and the other disciples had taken that attitude, it would have postponed Pentecost, maybe a hundred years. A preacher full of the Holy Spirit is not trying to destroy his brother. The fruits of the spirit are love, joy, and peace, remember?

So many saints have no joy because they come to the house of God looking at their watch. They come to the Lord's house wondering how soon they can get it over with.

Let me tell you something. There are a million Christians who have no joy. Why? Joy is a fruit of the Holy Spirit. Many a fundamentalist has no love. Why? He is not filled with the Holy Spirit. Many a Christian does not have the peace of God that passes all understanding, that could go with him down through the valley of the shadow of death. Why? He is not filled with the Holy Spirit.

Oh, we are so organized. We have our officers in church, but do we have what God is talking about? Do we have the fullness of the Holy Spirit? Do we have the fruits of the spirit? We can have the Spirit filled life.

Why Sit We Here Until We Die
2 Kings 7:3

I read this scripture in 2 Kings, chapter 7 years ago and many times since then. I have heard many sermons on this scripture. I have preached on this scripture many times. It always amazes me, the great lesson it contains. Today I would like to share it with you. This is a message to people who are caught in some awful power like sickness, fear, inner conflict, defeat failure hunger or poverty, etc. It is a message of hope to everyone who needs deliverance by the power of faith in God.

The whole city of Samaria was surrounded. The Syrian army had them encircled. They were hungry, so hungry, that it tells us in chapter 6, that they were eating their own children. A cry went up for the prophet Elisha to bring deliverance.

Elisha prophesied in twenty-four hours flour would sell for pennies. Not a man, woman or child, believed the prophecy; but Elisha lived close to God and knew God. Elisha waited on God. Some people do not believe in God's Word today. Some people just believe a part of God's Word. Some people do not believe in

154

God's power today. Some do not believe in God's concern for us today.

Outside of the gate were sitting four leprous men. They were sick, starving, and dying, surrounded by famine, and the Syrians. The people were helpless. As they sat at the entrance of the gate, they asked themselves a question. "Why sit we here until we die?"

How many times do people defeat themselves by torturing their minds with needless, unanswerable questions? When trouble, sickness or some calamity comes upon us we usually say, "Why did this happen to me?" "What have I done to deserve this?" There is only one question a human being should ask himself about his troubles, and that is, "Why sit I here until I die?" Who can explain the troubles, the afflictions, and the torments that come to us? Who has the answers to the why of man's sufferings? I do not have all the answers to the why. There is one thing I do know, however, and that is; we do not have to just sit still and die. We can rise up and do something about our situation. We can study God's Word. We can believe God's Word and trust in it. We can obey God's Word.

Friends, all of us have faith. We are all taught that in Romans 12:3, where Paul said, "God hath dealt to every man the measure of faith." We have the faith for the problems and situations in life. Why then do we sit and do nothing until we die? We can rise up and believe. Jesus said, "All things are possible to him that believeth." One of the things that we are prone to forget, when we are in trouble, is the presence of God is everywhere, at all times, to bless humanity.

The Bible says, "He that cometh to God must believe that He is and that He rewards them that diligently seek Him." (Hebrews 11:6) You can contact God anywhere at any time. The question we should ask ourselves is not, "Why has this happened to me?" or "What have I done to deserve it?" We should ask ourselves, "Why do we just sit here, doing nothing, until we die?"

In 2 Kings 7:3-4 three men reasoned that if they remained at the gate, they would die by famine, or if they entered the city, which was surrounded by the enemies, they would die because of the famine there. There was one hope and that was to rise up and march upon the Syrians. If the Syrians would receive them they would live. If they killed them they were going to die anyway.

That evening, while Samaria starved, these four skinny, sick hungry, dying men rose up, and in the twilight started their journey marching toward the Syrian army. They began their march of faith. Now can you see the picture of these four lepers? Four Men hungry, sick, dying, tired, full of pain, knowing that they be dead even before they reached the enemy, but it was hope, their only hope. Occasionally they would stagger and stumble and would have to help each other. What a picture we see, four men stumbling toward the enemy. They were not going to, just stand still and give up. If they were going to die, they would die as men of action and men with faith in their hearts. Maybe they didn't know it at the time, but God was leading them through their journey. Not only leading, but also going ahead of them.

Thousands of men with their horses and chariots were camped around the city of Samaria. They were in complete control of the city of Samaria. They were in complete control of the city when the four men made their march of faith. All the Syrians were sleeping, but remember God never sleeps. God saw four men coming. Each man was flesh and bones, but in their heart was faith; that was all God needed and wanted. God went to work. What can four defenseless, hopeless, sick men marching in the night hope to accomplish against a mighty army of the Syrians? It is not what four sick men can do; it is what God can do.

They are going forward on faith and trusting God. God made the faith march, of these four men, sound like a mighty army. What does the enemy hear and do? They hear thousands and thousands of men with their horses and chariots. The four men, so weak that they stumbled and fell every few steps, became the army of God. God made their stumbling sound like a million soldiers, like the hoof beats of thousands of horses. Sound like the wheels of thousands of chariots. Their whispers sounded like shouts of victory. Suddenly, the Syrians were awakened. They heard what appeared to be a mighty army. The Syrians arose and fled in the night, leaving everything behind.

The four men didn't know all this; they were going on their faith of desperation. They knew their only hope was in their faith. No doubt, they were afraid. They didn't know where the camp was. They only knew that it was out there somewhere in the darkness. None of these things stopped them because they were not willing to sit and die, without trying.

They did not know where the Syrians were located, "But God did." They did not know that they would ever make it to the camp, "But God did." They did not know that they weren't going to die on the way, "But God did." They did not know that their stumbling in the night would sound like a mighty army, horses, and Chariots, "But God did." They didn't know that Elisha had prophesied victory for the next day, "But God did." The four men did not know that they had to wait until the next day to get deliverance, so they obtained it the night before.

My friend, you do not have to wait until you have a better opportunity to be delivered. You do not have to wait until some one comes to your community praying for the sick to be healed. You do not have to wait until you are older, or until your circumstances change, or until you move to some other location in order to better your life. You do not have to wait at all. Rise up and make the march of faith and you can have deliverance now. You do not even have to wait until I get done with this sermon. Just raise your hands and heart to heaven and let your faith go and God will bless you all over, right now, just where you are.

The four men marched into the camp; they couldn't understand what had happened. They had not heard the army, horses, or chariots. Now the camp was empty and all around them was food, gold, silver, plenty for all.

Now they returned to Samaria, in triumph. They were able to run and shout that victory was theirs. The city was awakened, and the King was notified. By daylight the city of Samaria was full of food. The people were singing and dancing in the streets and the prophecy of Elisha had come to pass.

There was only one bad thing that happened in the whole affair. The man who mocked the prophecy of Elisha was appointed to man the gates, and he was trodden down under foot and killed, because of his doubt of what Elisha had said unto him, "Behold, thou shalt see it with thine eyes, but shalt not eat of thereof." He died without a morsel of food.

What was true back there is still true today. God has promised deliverance to all of us. God has promised to save us, to heal us, to prosper us, and to give us life. God has promised to give us more abundantly (John 10:10). Some doubt, and although they will see it with their own eyes, they will not partake of it. But those who believe it and reach out to receive it will be blest beyond their fondest dreams and expectations.

How many days this last year have you just sat waiting on something to happen to help your situation? How many years have you said, "God did it then, but things are different today?" How long has God's promises been available to you and you wouldn't accept them?

Elisha had the gift of the word of knowledge and discernment. (1 Cor 12:8) The four lepers sat. The four lepers moved. God had the plan, but did not put it into operation until they moved. They tried their own plan; but then God put His plan into them. God uses His people to carry out His plans.

The dictionary tells you that Christianity is a noun; but I want to tell you, in my thinking Christianity is a verb. Why, do I call it a verb? I call it a verb, because, Christianity is a religion of action. A Christian cannot sit still. You stop moving and sit still; you will miss all that God has planned for you. "Why sit you there until you die?"

What is Love
1 Corinthians 13

Jesus said, "You shall love the Lord your God with all your heart, and with all your soul, and with all your mind. This is the first and great commandment. And the second is like unto it, you shall love your neighbor as thyself."

> Love must come from the heart: All inward affection.
> Love must come from the body: All consciousness and all actions.
> Love must come from the mind: All thoughts.

These commandments are the sum of all, divine revelation and responsibility.

John 15:12: "This is My commandment, that you love one another, as I have loved you. Greater love has no man than this, that a man lay down his life for his friends." You are My friends, if you do whatsoever I command you. My commandment to you is the same as My Fathers commandment is to me. You love one another to the extent that I love you. I lay down My life for you;

you lay down your lives for each other. If you obey, you are My friend, if you do not obey, you are not. I am not going to make you bond slaves. I made you full partners and My personal representatives on earth,. You are to represent Me and reproduce My works as I represented God and did His works. So if you love someone, they do not become your slave or in bondage to you; but you become friends.

2 Corinthians 8:8: "Prove sincerity of your love." Never boastful, always honest, true and trustful.

Galatians 5: We are told by Paul that we are known by the service we give.

1 Peter 1:22: Seeing you have purified your souls in obeying the truth through the spirit unto unfeigned love of the brethren, see that you love one another with a pure heart fervently. (Don't be a hypocrite in your love; let your love be pure.)

1 John 1:18: John writes, "My little children, let us not love in word, neither in tongue; but in deed and in truth." Don't love by doctrine because you have to, but because you want to. Don't love by profession; but love in deed. Let your love be definite acts. Love in truth, by being genuine in profession and in deeds.

1 John 4:18: "There is no fear in love; but perfect love casts out fear, because fear has torment. He that fears is not made perfect in love." If you fear the judgment your love is not perfect.

1 Corinthians 8:1: tells us that love builds up; love does not tear down. And we find in **1 Corinthians 13:** "Love is patience, not hurry, love suffers long, believers hope and endures all things.

161

Love is generosity, not envious of jealous. Love is unselfishness, seeks only good for others. Love is good temper, never resentful. Love is humility, love in hiding. No parade, no airs, works then retires. Love is courtesy, does not behave unseemly, always polite, at home with all classes. Love is never rude or discourteous. Love is righteousness, love in conduct. Love is never glad when things go wrong for others. Love is sincerity. Love is always honest, just, joyful, and hopeful. Love is filling and fulfilling. Love at all times. Nothing can destroy divine love."

1 Peter 4:8: shows us the kind of love to have, "Have fervent (earnest, zealous, abundant) love among yourselves, for love shall over the multitude of sins." Not that our love will cause God to pass up or pardon the sins of others; that it will enable us to pass us the faults of others and not hold grudges ourselves. Do nothing merely because it is commanded, but do it from love to God and Man.

1 Thessalonians 4:8-9: "He that despises, despises not man, but God, who has also given unto us His Holy Spirit. But as touching brotherly love you need not that I write unto you; for you yourselves are taught of God to love one another." God teaches here of divine love among Christians. This God teaches by example of giving His only Son. This he did while we were yet rebels and enemies. God loved His enemies this much; surely Christians can love one another. He says here, "That we must increase our love of the brethren more and more."

Jesus asked Peter, "Do you love Me more than these?" Peter replies, "Yes Lord, You know that I love You." Jesus replies, "Then feed my lambs." Jesus said, "Do you love Me?" Peter

162

replied, yes Lord. Jesus said, "Feed My sheep." And Jesus said once more, "Simon, do you love Me?" Peter replies, "Lord, You know all things. You know that I love you." Jesus said, "Feed My sheep." Are His sheep hungry for your love? Feed His sheep. Ephesians 5:2: Paul writes, "Walk in love, as Christ also has loved us, and has given Himself for us as an offering and sacrifice to God for a sweet smelling savor." Can you give yourself for others? Can you give a part of yourself?

You can love wrong things. Do not get love confused with lust. Lust is not love. Man can love evil, man, the devil, or we can love God. You must love because you *want* to not because you *have* to. Make believe love is not true love. God wants you to choose to love Him. Love builds up. Love does not tear down. Learning to give. Learning to receive. This is the important thing. Love must center in the will, which is why love can be commanded and why God can command love.

Love's way is God's way. God commands us to love, and He gives us the way to accomplish it. That is His way. When God's way is placed in our hearts by the Holy Spirit, real love is known. By yielding your will to the will of God, and allowing the Holy Spirit to bring God's love into your relationship, you can love. Why should we do this? One reason, because God commands us to love.

Do we need a new church or a new heart?
Christ came not to condemn, but to save. This is love.
Love is spontaneous and divine.
Love is when two are one.
Love is eternal and caring.
Love is the Golden Rule.

GRANDPA'S LESSONS ABOUT JESUS

Love is sharing.
Love is Christ in you.
Love is talking things out.
Love is bearing.
Love is hearing.
Love is trusting.
Love is being a friend when things go right and even when
things go wrong.
Love must be wanted,
Love is the cure for all things.
Love completes all things.
Love is giving and forgiving.
Love is filling and fulfilling.
Love is inward and outward affection.
Love is complete, heart, body, and mind.
Love is being honest, true, and trustful.
Love is reflected in your actions and your talk.
Love is being wanted to love.
Love is building up, not tearing down.
Love cures all things.
Love is feeling joy when others feel joy.
Love is hurting when others are hurting.
Love is sorrow when others sorrow.
Love is rejoicing in success, when both you and others succeed.
Love is standing by someone when they fail.
Love is the freely giving of one's self for the benefit of another.

Christian Love is the secret of a happy life.

Mary Magdalene's Easter
The Resurrection Of Jesus

Easter means many different things to many people. To some it may mean a time when families come together. To others it may mean new hats and clothing. Then you have the ones that it means Bunnies, Easter rabbits and candy eggs. Yet to others something far different...

John 20:1-18, we see in the text today, we have the meaning of Easter, for Mary Magdalene, the woman who, in time past, Jesus had cast out seven devils. To Mary it was a time of excitement. We learn of her excitement as she approached the tomb and saw the stone rolled away. She was amazed to find Jesus gone when she looked inside. Having arrived at the tomb before anyone sunrise, she decided to wait, maybe someone would come who could tell her where they had taken Him. Maybe the gardener would tell her where He is when he comes to the garden.

Christianity is based upon the Resurrection. We cannot understand with our worldly minds the Creation or the virgin birth, we know there are many eyewitness accounts of the

Resurrection, and it does provide us with an understanding of God's plan.

You may be asking, "Didn't Mary Magdalene know that Jesus would raise from the dead?" What happens here is something like reading the novel where the villain is fighting a seemingly winning battle with the good man of the house. The story continues, but I can't wait until tomorrow to find the outcome, so I turn to the end and read where the villain is destroyed and the good man becomes the hero.

Mary came and saw, but she did not understand. Peter came, but John came faster and they returned home. Mary stayed to seek her Lord. Mary was weeping when she turned and saw Jesus. Jesus said, "Why do you weep Mary?" When Jesus spoke, Mary recognized Him. Mary knew Jesus. Jesus said, "Mary, go and tell." Mary obeyed the Lord.

What did Easter conclude for Mary Magdalene? Three things:
1. **Joy:** Christ has always been the victor. Here Jesus brings immortality to light, because He is alive, not dead. Because peace is a reality (read John 14:27) Jesus says, "I am leaving you with a gift, peace of mind and heart. And the peace I give isn't fragile like the peace the world gives, so don't be troubled or afraid."
2. **Hope:** Here on earth, and in the life beyond. "If only in this world we have hope, we are of all men most miserable. We have hope of eternal life in the presence of Christ. Separation by death is not final, but a passageway to God." Jesus says, "Let not your hearts be troubled...."
3. **Witness:** Mary could not keep silent, she ran, in her excitement to tell the others that she had seen Jesus, and

GRANDPA'S LESSONS ABOUT JESUS

He is alive. The church was born, and the good news was spread. Magdalene received the commission to spread the news of His ascension. She came and told what He said.

So what is the conclusion of Easter? It is Joy, and the witness of the ever- living Christ. It is victory over sin, death, and the grave.

What have you received from Easter? What is your conclusion of Easter? Through Easter can you really see the plan of God, or will we just "go home again?" Will we say, "I don't believe it, I do not really know for sure, but I hope so?" May the resurrection of our Lord and Savior, Jesus Christ, bring immortality to light for you this day and forever, that you may have joy, hope and be continuing witness for Him.

Death frightens some, spooks others, and some just do not understand it, and that is why we are so uncomfortable with death. But Jesus, the Son of God, came back from the dead. Jesus took all of the spookiness out of it. Jesus made His appearance in the daylight, in the open air, not just once but several times, even in broad daylight. Jesus appeared in many different places.

Some said, "It must be a ghost" and they fled with fright. Can you blame them? It is one thing to see a ghost in the cemetery, but quite different to see a friend on Sunday morning, who died on Friday coming up to you and speaking to you with a voice that you recognize. He asks you to touch him and handle him to prove your doubts, and then he eats some food that he prepared with his own hands.

Jesus said He would conquer death, and here He is alive and well to prove it. They had been inclined to believe His claim. Now they know. Now they can tell the world for sure. It wasn't very long until they were out telling everyone. Nothing on earth could stop them.

What changed these ordinary men, these one-time cowards, who were afraid to stand too near the cross for fear of being involved? What changed these witnesses into hero's, the ones who would stop at nothing? What changed them, was it a séance? Was it a swindle? Was it a Hallucination, spooky nonsense in a dark room? No my friends, it was none of these, but it was somebody quietly doing what He said He would do. Walk right through death.

I know my redeemer lives because we have proof through history and through God's Word. Christianity is built upon the experiences of men who knew Jesus personally in the flesh and bear witness that God raised Jesus from the dead. I know my redeemer lives because of the Lord's Day; Jesus rose the first day of the week. For almost 2000 years the first day of the week has been observed as the Lord's Day, a day of rest and worship.

I know my redeemer lives because the New Testament is a vital witness to Christ's resurrection. The remarkable fact is not only that Christ rose from the dead, but that His resurrection was knowable to His disciples. They saw Him die. They placed His body in the tomb, made secure with the Roman seal and guarded by Roman soldiers. When Christ burst the bands of death asunder, those very Roman soldiers became as dead men. The New Testament is the account of "that which men have heard, which they have seen with their own eyes, which they have looked upon and their hands have handled of the word of life."

GRANDPA'S LESSONS ABOUT JESUS

I know my redeemer lives because the Holy Communion is a continuing witness to the resurrection of Jesus Christ, our ever-living savior and Lord. Our remembrance is not that of a Nazarene carpenter, but of the resurrection of the living Christ.

He is the regenerative power of history. Something happened that changed the character of that little group of fearful disciples and changed he whole course of history. Prior to the resurrection Christ's disciples fled to escape persecution and death. After the resurrection they met death unafraid. The resurrection was knowable to men just like our selves. You too may know Him and the power of His resurrection.

I know that my redeemer lives, and because He lives, I too, shall live. I know my redeemer lives, because of a woman called Mary Magdalene, a sinner like myself, one who Christ forgave, like myself, one that Jesus touch, like myself.

I know my redeemer lives because I have talked to Him and He has talked to me. I have heard Him, and I have listened to Him and He has listened to me. I have felt Him. There is no doubt in me, whatsoever, so when I pass on, remember I want you to rejoice, rejoice I say, for I know my redeemer lives and I shall live also. Praise His Holy Name.

May the peace of God, which passes all understanding, keep your hearts and minds in the knowledge and love of God, and of his Son, Jesus Christ our Lord. May the blessings of God Almighty, the Father, the Son, and the Holy Spirit, be among and within you, and remain with you always. In Jesus' Name we do pray. Amen.

Jesus Is Not For Sale

One day the disciples began praying for some new Christians to receive the Holy Spirit, for they had only been baptized in the name of Jesus. Then Peter and John laid their hands upon the believers and they received the Holy Spirit, others were healed.

There was an unbeliever named Simon there and saw all of this. After seeing this Simon offered the disciples money if they would give Simon this power. Simon said, "Come on, I will pay you well, just give me this power. Show me how you do all this." But Peter said, "Your money perish with you. Don't even think God's gift can be bought. You cannot buy even a part of this, because your heart is not right with God. Repent and maybe God will yet forgive your evil thoughts." (Acts 8:15-22)

I was in town the other day and saw a sign that read "All ladies jeans on sale one half off," which made me think of this scripture. My friends, Christ is not on sale. People seem to think if you can't buy it, it has no value. Jesus Christ is free. You can keep all you have. Jesus paid the price on the cross of Calvary. I tell you friend, turn everything you have over to Jesus and you will still get the bargain of your life. You can't purchase salvation, because the price has already been paid. Yet you have to give your all for eternity with God. What a bargain.

You sincerely repent of your sins and Jesus forgives. What a bargain it is! You have a need for an ear and Jesus listens to you. What a bargain! Jesus is a good listener. You listen, and Jesus talks. What a bargain! You will be surprised to hear what Jesus has to say to you if you will but listen. Jesus talks in many different ways.

If we would buy, how and when would we buy? Would you buy and then put it upon a shelf, and let it lay until you decided you needed it? Would you put a little money down, then put it in lay away until you could pay the rest? Would you wait until it went on sale? Maybe you would buy it on credit. I want it now, but I will pay for it later. I will buy now and pay later.

Budget your life also. If you want to be a success you must budget and plan your income, likewise your life, you must plan your life and handle it with care. Budget your income, your work, your play, but you cannot budget God. Christianity is a full time duty. It is a way of life. You can't budget Christianity to use only on a Sunday; it must be a full time commitment.

Is your Christian life like an automobile? Get it and put it in the garage. We want it only when we need it. Do we want Jesus only when we need Him? The automobile, we want it ready and willing to jump and go when we do. Do we expect Jesus to jump and come to our aid, only the times we need Him?

Jesus is our servant, yes, yet He is our King. What a bargain.

171

GRANDPA'S LESSONS ABOUT JESUS

(Read John 10:10-18) Christ is the best bargain you will ever receive.

You cannot buy true friendship. You cannot buy salvation. You cannot buy a wife or a husband or their love and you cannot buy Jesus Christ, for He is not for sale. He is free, because He has already paid the price. Why did God make such a plan in the beginning?

It is not the size of your bank account. It is the size of your heart. Jesus never asks you how much money you have every time you ask Him to do something for you. But Jesus said, "Do you love Me?" "Do you love Me?" "Do you love me more than your possessions?" "Do you love Me more than any thing else in the world?"

James said, "Faith not works is what Jesus is looking for." You don't deserve it. You are not worthy of it. You can't earn it. All the money in the world can't buy it. So what are we going to do?

The choice is yours. It is free. It is a gift from God. It has already been paid for. Jesus is a bargain at full price. He's your all. Do you really realize what it cost Jesus for your salvation? The price is paid. Jesus paid that price on Calvary.

God gave us life. In the beginning God also gave each of us a will, the freedom of choice. We must choose this day who we will serve, God or Satan. The choice is yours. Salvation is free. Jesus paid the price.

Come, repent and believe. How simple. How easy. How free.

Christians Are God's Children

In the book of, Mark 10:14 Jesus said, "Let the little children come unto me for such is the kingdom of Heaven." We must become as a little child to enter the Kingdom of God. We are to be children of God first, and then we are to grow in His Word, in His Way, and in the end become adults in his Way.

I would like to try and show you the difference in children and adult, thinking and living. I would like to show you how children think and how adults think. When a child is first born, the child will accept things as they are. Adults very seldom accept in their entirety and say that is not for today, or dad and mom did not do it that way. Children immediately believe what their parents teach them. Adults want to argue and say, "That cannot be." Children trust completely in dad and mom. Adults will say; trust in what? If it is free it must not be worth anything. Children love completely and immediately. Adults love usually worldly things more than spiritually things. Children forgive and forget. Adults say they forgive, but hold a grudge, maybe for weeks or months. Children, when parents are happy, they are happy. Children are optimists. Adults, something is wrong or will go wrong, on the pessimist side. Children feel safe and secure in their father's hands. Adults have tension and uneasiness, and cannot completely give themselves over to their Heavenly Father. Children feel that everything their parents have is theirs. Adults do not realize, everything their Heavenly Father has made, He made for them. Children have happy faces. It is easy to make a child smile. I see some adults that haven't smiled in years. Children have compassion for each other and their parents, they laugh when their parents laugh, they cry when their parents cry. Adults say, "Well they deserved it, or let him take care of himself. Of course we could go on and on.

What I am trying to say to you is this; we are children of God, when we accept Jesus, no matter what age we are. God expects us to grow spiritually as we expect our children to grow, mentally, physically, and spiritually. God expects us to accept His Word for what it says, God expects us to grow on His Word, not on some tradition or ritual developed by man or a denomination to fill their own need.

God is our Father. Jesus is our Lord. The Holy Spirit comes to teach and to lead us. We must be born again to enter the kingdom of God, the Kingdom of Heaven. Believers increase in knowledge. This is what God's Word tells us. Unbelievers go into more darkness and ignorance. Paul says, "If they wish to remain ignorant, let them."

John 3:1-7 teaches us, "Ye must be born again." One birth is a begetting and a coming into existence. The second birth is an adoption to become the sons and daughters of God. We either live after the flesh or after the Spirit. In John 3:8 "As the natural man hears the wind, so the man born again hears the voice of the Spirit."

Do we know what this new birth is? Millions do not know this new birth and even Nicodemus, a very learned and religious man, did not know what Jesus was talking about. What Jesus was saying is "When you accept Jesus as your Lord and Savior, you become as a child spiritually." When you are a child, Paul says we must start on milk, then bread, then after that meat. We do not learn it all at once. As like we grow physically, we must grow spiritually. The more we learn from God and His Word, the more we grow toward adulthood.

Romans 1:19-20 states that there is no excuse for men to be ignorant of the invisible things. All invisible things, even the eternal power of God are clearly seen by the visible things of creation.

Let us get back of being born again for a minute. Being born again means to have the Spirit Baptism, which is the new birth. Now what does it mean to have the Spirit Baptism? Let us look at John 7:37-39, at the end of the holidays He says called out to the people, "If anyone thirst, let him come unto Me and drink. For the Scriptures tell us that rivers like living waters shall flow out from the inner most being of anyone of us who believes in Him." Here Jesus was speaking of the Holy Spirit, who would be given to all that believed in Him, but we must realize that the Holy Spirit would not be given until Jesus returns to His Glory in God's Kingdom.

Let me give you four conditions for the Spirit Baptism:

1. Thirst, this means craving and passion of the soul for

complete union with God and the fullness of the Spirit. We do become one in Christ.

2. Come unto Me. This means the complete surrender of the life to do the whole will of God. It does not mean just do a part here and a part there.

3. Drink. This means the wholehearted reception into one's life of the gifts, the fruits and operations of the Holy Spirit. Drink in all that God, Jesus, and the Holy Spirit has to offer you.

4. Believe. Believe on Me as the Scriptures has said. This means believe in and obey to the letter the whole gospel program.

Do all four and then you will receive. Then what will happen? Then out of the believer will flow, unlimited power, to do the works of Christ. John 4:13-15 and John 4: 21-24. Also take to read John 14:12-13. Out of the belly means, the innermost being, the soul and the spirit. Remember this living water is the Holy Spirit, John 7:39.

The Christian it says has Power of Attorney. It says he that believeth in Me. He that believeth is every one that believes, not just the disciples only. There will be a constant flow from the believer without measure as Christ experienced. Living water has to flow. Likewise the Holy Spirit has to flow. As I told you Christianity is a religion of action, it cannot stand still.

The rivers of living water refers to the fullness of the Holy Spirit that was to be given to all men after Jesus had become glorified, after Jesus has returned to His Father.

Do you get what I am saying? I am talking to you as a friend. I hope you realize that. God gave me a message just for you. I just want to point you toward Heaven. There is only one way; you must be born again, born again by the Word of God. It must be a talk between you and Jesus, between you and God. You must change because of God.

You must become as little children. You must accept, believe, trust, love, forgive, and have compassion. Do you really know Jesus? Do you really know God? Or do you Just hope you do?

Have you been born again? Do you have that living water? Do you have the fullness of the Holy Spirit? If you do not know if you have been born again, then chances are you have not. If you do not know for sure that you have been saved, then chances are, you have not.

You must be born again, because Jesus said so. You must become as little children, because Jesus said so. I joke with you outside of the church. Right now, today, I have never more serious than I am right now. Let us stand in honor before God today. Let us face Him in honor at the Gates of the Kingdom of Heaven.

What Is Man?
Psalms 8:1-9

In Genesis 1:26-28 God said, "Let us make man in our image, after our likeness; and let them have dominion over the fish of the sea and the fowl of the air, and over the cattle, and over all the earth and over every creeping thing that creeps upon the earth."

"So God created man in His own image, in the image of God created He Him; male and female created He them. And God blessed them, and God said unto them; be fruitful and multiply, and replenish the earth, and subdue it; and have dominion over the fish of the sea and over the fowl of the air, and over every living thing that moves upon the earth."

Now God tells us how he made man. Genesis 2:7 states, "And the Lord God formed man of the dust of the ground, and breathed into his nostrils the breath of life, and man became a living soul." So we see here, God made the body of dust. Man still was nothing more, and God breathed into him the breath of Life, then man became a living soul.

178

GRANDPA'S LESSONS ABOUT JESUS

So, I want you to understand, Man is not a body with a mind and a spirit; but man is a living spirit, with a mind and a body. The real you, is not the Body we see, but the real you is the mind and spirit that lives in that body.

The body is wonderfully made. Let us look at the body of man. The body consists of chemicals, iron, sugar, salt, carbon, iodine, phosphorus, lime, calcium, and many others.

The body has 206 bones, 600 muscles, 970 miles of blood vessels, 400 cups on the tongue, 10,000 nerves and branches, lungs that inhale 2,400 gallons of air daily, and a telephone system that relates to the brain instantly any known sound, taste, sight, touch or smell. The heart will beat 4,200 times an hour and pumps 12 tons of blood daily.

The soul of man is the seat of his emotions, passions, desires, appetites, and all feelings.

Man's spirit is the seat of the intellect, will and conscience. It is capable of all divine powers only in a lesser degree. The inner man, consisting of the soul and spirit is eternal. Man was made a little lower than angels. We were created sinless, but capable of sin. Man was made consisting of a body, mind and spirit. Our flesh is different from all other creatures. Man was created with two natures; worldly and spiritual natures are clearly distinguished in scripture. The soul and spirit are not dust. The spirit leaves the body at death. The body can be killed, but the spirit cannot be killed, it lives on forever through eternity. Both body and spirit were made to glorify God. The inner man is eternal. The body is mortal.

Souls (minds) and the spirits of a righteous person go to Heaven and the body goes to the grave. Souls (minds) of the wicked will end up in hell while their bodies go to the grave and return to dust.

The body is the house of the inner man, our dwelling place, while here on earth. Man has a will making him in every sense a free mortal agent and responsible being. Free to choose his direction and what he should do every day of his life.

Only Satan or his followers can cause you to sin. Sin was a voluntary act of the divine will and the elevation of the will of man over the will of God. Sin came through a denial of the divine will and the elevation of the will of man over the will of God. Sin came through unbelief of God's Word. Sin came through rebellion against God's Word.

When sin came in man fell. When man fell man became:
1. Separated from God.
2. Ignorant and Blind.
3. Evil in conscious.
4. Corrupt and deceitful in heart.
5. Evil in thoughts.
6. Lustful and ungodly.
7. Dominated by Satan.
8. Dead in sin.
9. Subject to suffering and death.
10. Cursed of God to hard labor.
11. Sinners by birth.
12. Subject to sickness, disease, pain, and all present evils.
13. Short lived.

God has given the revelation of Himself, His creation, and all of His plans for man, so that man might know his origin, present responsibility, and destiny. The Bible is the record of this revelation.

God appraises man as the highest of creation. You are worth more than the whole world to Him. What is man's destiny? Man charts his own destiny by his conforming or by not conforming to the Gospel. Eternal life with God in Heaven and on earth is the destiny of these who conform to truth. Eternal hell and punishment are the destiny of those who refuse to obey truth.

But as we study God's Word we find that God has everything under control.

In the beginning God gave man everything he would ever need. Man sinned against God, doubted God and believed Satan. God spoke through His prophets. God spoke directly to them, and man rejected God. So God sent His Son. What did man do? Man killed God's Son. Jesus died for your sins and for my sins. Jesus promised you power, if you followed Him. Then after Jesus ascended into Heaven, He sent to us the Holy Spirit. The Holy Spirit came and taught man by living in him, dwelling in you, God's Temple.

Now God says, "It is up to you." What have you done? What will you do? What do you intend to do? There are only a few real godly men on earth. Do you know what to do? We must become acquainted with God to find peace within our self and by studying and believing His Word. We must return to God.

Will you tell others about God? Will you sit home and feel sorry for yourself and others? Will you so live your life that others will see Christ in you? What is man that God is so mindful of him? You have an appointment to die. You have an inescapable appointment with God. You will stand before Jesus and confess that He is Lord, the Son of God.

The Word tells you that the good and bad will be separated in the next life.

God has promised to you:

1. Salvation: That if you shall confess within your mouth the Lord Jesus, and shall believe in your heart that God has raised Him from the dead you shall be saved. For with the heart man believes unto righteousness; and with the mouth confession is made unto salvation.
2. Prosperity: Keep the charge of the Lord, to walk in His ways. That you may prosper in all that you do. The hand of God is upon all them for good that seek Him; but His power and His wrath are against them that forsake Him. If they obey and serve Him, they shall spend their days in prosperity, and their years in pleasure. I wish above all things that you might prosper as your soul prospers. What is prosperity?
3. Health and wealth.
4. All wants and needs; you shall not want any good thing. What ever you shall ask the Father, in My Name, believing He will give to you, ask the Father in My Name, He will give it to you. What ever we ask, we receive of him.

God created man and never left him alone. Here is some ways that God visits man:

GRANDPA'S LESSONS ABOUT JESUS

1. Coming Himself.
2. Sending Christ.
3. Sending the Holy Spirit.
4. Sending Angels.
5. By prophets.
6. Dreams and Visions.
7. By His Word.

Jesus said, "I will never leave you alone. Lo, I am with you always."

What is man that God is mindful of him?

Hey! Cheer up. Be happy. Smile. Get Zeal back into your life. Don't forget to live; life is a gift from God. God loves you. He wants you happy, joyful and with happy faces. What is man?

Man is God's pride and joy.
Man is God's companion.
Man is the love of God.
Man is a spirit, with a mind and body.
Man is a being that lives forever.
Man is one who belongs to God.
Man is worth more than the whole world to God.

What is man that God is mindful of him? Know yourself.

Freedom

We want freedom from what? Do we want freedom from Emperors, Kings, or of Laws? Or do we want freedom of press, religion, and speech? Did we come to America to get freedom, from and for all these things? Speaking of coming to a new country, you hear people say that we brought our religion, our God over here to America, but let me tell you what I believe. I believe that God brought us here to America, to a land where we could build on Christianity, on His Word and His Way. That is how our forefathers started this country.

What I want to talk about to you today is the most important freedom you can receive and that is freedom from your old master; sin. Paul said that we should not be slaves to sin, but to our new master righteousness. We should be obedient to the ways of God. Paul says, "The wages of sin is death, but the free gift of God is eternal life, through Jesus Christ our Lord."

With freedom goes responsibility. You have a new master. Before you were free to do what you wanted to do. Now you are still free to do what you want to do; but you no longer want to do the things you once did.

In verse 19 Paul writes, "Because of the weakness of your flesh, as you have yielded your bodily members to sin and uncleanness, you must now do likewise to righteousness and Godliness. You must make a change."

In verse 20 Paul again emphasizes the fact that a man cannot be a saint and a sinner; holy and sinful; and cannot serve God and Satan, or be a servant of sin and righteousness at the same time.

In verse 21 Paul uses fruits to refer to good and evil results.
Sin has two main results:
1. Presents shame and emptiness.
2. Future, eternal death and hell, the end of a life of sowing to the flesh.

Now, in the present life men are free from sin in Christ. A change in masters means a change in service.
Righteousness has two main results:
1. Present holiness to life.
2. Future and eternal life, the end of a life of sowing to the spirit.

Verse 23 "Divine justice is under obligation to give sinners their wages or be in debt to them forever. Eternal life is a free gift. Men merit hell, but not eternal life Jesus Christ alone procured it and gives it freely to all of those who believe. For the wages of sin is death; but the gift of God is eternal life, through Jesus Christ."

John 8:31-36 tells us about freedom. Free from the law. The law will kill you. If you are condemned according to the law you are guilty. You deserve death according to the law; but Jesus freed you from the law unto grace. Law was made to judge the guilty. Jesus came to set you free if you will continue in My Word. If, expresses a condition, "If you will continue in My Word." The condition to be met if these new believers were to remain as true disciples and have freedom from sin was "Continue in My Word." For if any man "commits sin, he is the servant of sin."

This is the secret of freedom from sin, sickness, and all the curses of this life that Christ died to set men free from. No man can commit sin and not be a servant of sin. No man can sin and not have to pay the penalty for sin and what did Paul say the penalty of sin was? "The wages of sin is death." The servant of sin does not abide in the house of the Lord forever; but if we become free from sin we will abide with the Son of God in God's house forever.

If the Son makes one free from sin, he is free indeed, and is no longer a servant of the sin. Jesus says, "Therefore if the Son shall make you free, you shall be free indeed." So we are seeking independence from what? We are seeking freedom from what? Jesus just told us we are seeking independence from Satan. We are seeking freedom from Satan, from sin, and all the things that destroy us.

In Luke 4:15-21 it says here that we were in trouble, "But Jesus came," and with Jesus came freedom. Jesus came with the same freedom then, two thousand years ago, that men today are seeking.

It was the custom for Jesus to go to the house of God on the

Sabbath. It was the custom every Sabbath for 7 persons to read, a priest, a Levite, and 5 ordinary Israelites. It was the custom that all readers of scriptures stand while reading and praying, which was a mark of respect to God and to His Word.

Jesus opened the Book and read: "The Spirit of the Lord is upon me; because He has anointed Me to preach the Good News to the poor. He has sent Me to heal the brokenhearted and to set the captives free. He has sent Me to make the blind see, and to set at liberty them that are bruised and to preach the acceptable year of the Lord."

Jesus said that He had a two-fold ministry:
 1. He was appointed to preach:
    A. The Gospel (good news) to the poor, needy, destitute.
    B. Deliverance to captives in sin, sickness and death.
    C. The acceptable year or period when liberty was proclaimed to all people on the Day of Atonement. (Jesus is that liberty.) When the atonement of Christ is fully embraced, the sick, sinful, helpless, and needy are restored to health, holiness, power and prosperity, and have full dominion over Satan and membership and communion in God's Family.

 2. He was appointed to heal:
    A. Heal the broken in heart, mind (soul) and body.
    B. The blind in body, soul, and spirit. Those in darkness.
    C. The bruised, the completely crushed and shattered in life. The oppressed and broken.

And God's Word says, "And He closed the Book of Isaiah, and gave it to the Minister and sat down." Jesus said, "This day is this scripture fulfilled in your ears." He was saying, "You have been seeking independence, you have been seeking freedom, you have been seeking liberty. This day it has come unto you, if you will accept it."

So we can celebrate the independence of our country and try to get freedom in the laws; but first we must get our freedom from Satan. We must listen to the Word of God that was preached by Jesus and is here with us today. We must free ourselves from Satan that we can be healed of a broken heart. We must listen to the preaching of deliverance, or receiving or recovering our sight. And to set free those that are bruised.

In 2 Kings 7:3 we read where the time Elisha and the Israelites were surrounded by the Syrians. There were four leprous men at the entering of the gate; and they said to one another, "Why sit we here until we die, arise let us go forth and let us get this freedom." Let us get this independence that we seek and desire. Jesus has it for us. But you must reach out to get it.

Today people have a tendency to divide the ministry. They call one preacher a deliverance minister, the other a pastor. I only read of one kind of ministry in the Bible. That is a deliverance ministry. A Holy Ghost ministry is a deliverance ministry. The church is here for only one main purpose, and that is to deliver the oppressed and set them free. Jesus died on the cross for one purpose, for the prison doors to swing open, that the captives go free.

The ministry that Jesus had is the only ministry that we find will work for the people today. That is the only ministry Jesus or the Apostles preached. That is what the early church had.

GRANDPA'S LESSONS ABOUT JESUS

Each sermon Jesus preached was a "pill," "a dose of medicine." It was a sermon to set you free. Here was what Jesus said:

- Pray
- Learn
- Pray
- Teach
- Pray
- Exhort
- Pray
- Give your all
- Pray
- Serve
- Pray

These were Jesus' instructions 2000 years ago and they are the same today. Jesus said, "Feed My sheep, set them free." Jesus said, "Feed My lambs, set them free."

If you have the Holy Spirit, you have something to give the people. You can't just make people believe that you have the Holy Ghost. Satan will throw you in a state of confusion, and you will confuse them about you. What did Jesus command us do? Jesus commanded them to receive the power of the Holy Spirit. He said if we love Him to keep His commandments and He will send us the Holy Spirit.

What did He command them to do? He commanded them to preach, to heal the sick by God's power, to cast out devils. He commanded us to do the same thing He did. Jesus was thinking of you when He said the believer could do the works, which Jesus did. As He was so are we in this world. He set us an example that we should follow his steps. We are to take up the ministry where He left off. He was the light of the world. Now, Jesus said, you are the light of the world. Jesus said the promise is unto you and to your children, to all that are afar off, even as many as the Lord our God shall call. If you have been called out of sin the promise of this power is unto you.

We ask for freedom. God wants to give us freedom. Do we really want to be free?

What is wrong with the present church set-up today? Why do so many preachers have ulcers or they have a nervous break down? I will tell you why. It is because a part of the church is out of order.

If a sheep is fed he will come back again.

What is freedom? Here it is in God's Word. Jesus said, "I have come to set you free and if I set you free, you are free indeed. Do you have your freedom? Do you want freedom? Jesus says to you: "Come unto me all you that labor and are heavy laden and I will give you rest. Take My yoke upon you and learn of Me for I am meek and lonely in heart, for My yoke is easy and My burden is light."

In closing I want you to remember the words of Paul, "The wages of sin is death, but the gift of God is eternal life, through Jesus Christ our Lord." He said through Jesus Christ our Lord.

In The Garden

Let us take a walk with Jesus through the garden this morning, through the Garden of Gethsemane.

In meditating upon God's Word we have met Jesus in several places. As a babe in Bethlehem's manger, healing the lame, raising the dead, making the blind see, stilling the waves, and casting out demons. Let us meet Him in the Garden of Gethsemane. Here it is that we see Him as we should.

In Matthew 26:36-46, we read: "Then Jesus went with them to a place called Gethsemane, then He said to His disciples, 'Sit here, while I go yonder and pray.' And then talking to Peter and James and John, He began to be sorrowful and troubled. Then Jesus said to them, 'My soul is very sorrowful, even to death, remain here and watch with Me.' And going a little farther, He fell on His face and prayed, 'My Father, if it be possible, let this cup pass from Me; nevertheless not as I will, but as Thou wilt.' And Jesus returned to the disciples and found them sleeping, and He said to Peter, 'So could you not watch with Me one hour? Watch and pray that you may not enter into temptation; the spirit indeed is willing, but the flesh is weak.' Again, for the second time, Jesus went away and prayed, 'My Father, if this cannot pass unless I drink it, Thy will be done.' Again He came and found them sleeping, for their eyes were heavy. So, leaving them again, He went away and prayed for the third time. Saying the same words. Then He came to the disciples and said to them, 'Are you still sleeping and taking your rest? Behold the hour is at hand, and the Son of man is betrayed into the hands of sinners. Rise let us be going; see, My betrayer is at hand.'"

First of all let us see Jesus in the conflict, which He experienced. He took with Him His disciples. He told eight of them to sit at the edge of the garden, while He went and prayed yonder. But He said to Peter, James and John, "You three come with Me for My soul is exceeding sorrowful, even unto death; tarry here, and watch with Me."

These three had witnessed His transfiguration, and now they witnessed His agony in the garden. We see Jesus here praying unto His Father, "O My Father if it be possible, let this cup pass from Me; nevertheless, not My will but Your Will be done."

The idea here is to be that the devil tried to kill Christ before He could get to the cross, but God heard His prayer and saved Him from death. If Satan could succeed in killing Christ any time from infancy to the cross, he could defeat God's plan of redemption. Christ had to get to the cross where He spoiled Satan's powers and triumphed over them.

The cup refers to His cup of death on the cross.

Watch and pray, for indeed the "spirit" is willing, but the "flesh" is weak. Again He prayed, "O Father, My Father, if this cup may not pass from Me, except I drink it, Your will be done." Again He finds His disciples sleeping. He prayed the third time. (Showing that we must be persistent in our prayers.) The time has come, the hour is at hand, and the Son of man is betrayed into the hands of sinners. Rise, let us be going; behold He is at hand, that betrays Me.

As we walk through the garden we see Jesus in the conflict, which He experienced. Shuddering with fear and trembling because:
   A. Wrath of God poured out upon Him.
   B. Every sin from Adam's to Judgment day.
   C. Agony awaiting the crucifixion.
   D. He who knew no sin, tasted death for all.
   E. Rulers of the land were all against Him.
   F. His own followers were to betray Him.

Here it is that we see Jesus, true-man, true-God. He feels the indescribable agony as man, and by divine strength He was able to endure it.

In the garden I know the consolation that He gives:
   A. He overcame the world, flesh, and the devil, by "Thy will be done."
   B. He was wounded, for my transgressions. He was bruised for my iniquities.
   C. God placed my sins upon Him where they rightfully belonged. (He is my sin bearer.)
   D. He took them to the cross. He died because of them.
   E. Trusting in this death He saves me and will help me in temptation.

Here I have release. (He took my sins away.)
Here I have assurance. (As I trust in Him, He helps me.)
Here I have contentment. (I am weak, but He is strong.)

To possess this consolation I must conduct myself in the same manner, which He demonstrates, while I experience conflict:

A. Pattern of prayer: "Thy will be done."
   1. Relationship: "O my Father."
   2. Request: "If it be possible," I must pray God's will for all bodily wants.
   3. Response: "Never the less not as I will, but as you will."
   4. Recognition: Impossible, some things God cannot grant, it is not His will. We must recognize this or we will become disappointed in Him.
   5. Repetition: Jesus persisted in prayer. Three times on the same subject.
   6. Ratification: Saying the same words. Our repeating has been confirmed in the mind of God, and to our satisfaction, we know that He knows what we have desired.

What do we learn from Jesus having met Him in the garden?

In my life, sin always makes me sad, but I can leave them with Jesus, God hath laid my sin and iniquity upon Him who is my sin-bearer. Sin makes me to fear, but my consolation remains in the fact that He overcame it for me. This consolation can be mine if I conduct myself in the manner in which He did in the garden of Gethsemane.

My Question is that of the unknown songwriter:

GRANDPA'S LESSONS ABOUT JESUS

Have you been in the garden with Jesus,
Alone with the Savior in prayer"
Did the Angels of Heaven come near you,
Was Jesus awaiting you there?

Have you been in the garden with Jesus?
O! say have you tarried in prayer
Till the angels of Heaven met you there,
with Jesus, the Savior, in prayer?

When you meet with conflict, temptation, that would overcome
you, go to Jesus for release, for assurance, and for contentment.

Jesus says, "Watch and pray, that you enter not into temptation."
Would you meet Jesus in the garden? If so you must submit
your will to Him.

My Lord, My God
John 20:19-31

Here we see Jesus appears to the ten disciples. Judas had killed himself and Thomas went home feeling sorry for himself. Now on Sunday, the doors were shut and locked for fear of the Jews. Not the Romans but fear of the Jews. Now Jesus appeared unto them. Jesus came and stood in the midst of them and said, "Peace be unto you." This proves that resurrected bodies do not need openings to get into homes. They are called "spiritual bodies." They are spiritual beings that can appear and disappear at will. The laws of the world, the laws of nature, or laws of science, do not apply to the resurrected body.

Jesus chose Sunday to appear to His disciples. He also chose Sunday to send the Holy Spirit baptism upon them. Jesus also resurrected on Sunday, so Sunday became the Sabbath for the Christian. They were gathered here, perhaps in the upper room where they had eaten the Passover feast with Jesus just a few days before.

Then all at once Jesus appeared unto them saying, "Peace be

unto you." This was the common salutation of Hebrews. Jesus said, "My peace, I give unto you. Let not your hearts be troubled, neither let it be afraid." Jesus showed them His hands, His feet, and His side. Then the disciples were glad, when they saw the Lord.

Jesus said, "My Father sent Me into the world for a purpose. Now I send you to continue on with the same work, for the same purpose. You have the same power and the same fullness of the spirit that the Father gave to Me." Then Jesus breathed upon them and said, "Receive you the Holy Spirit. I give you the power to bind and to loose and to do the works that I did."

But the Word says that Thomas was not with them when Jesus came. The other disciples went to Thomas and said, "We have seen the Lord." Thomas said, "Except I shall see in His hands the print of the nails, and put my finger into the prints of the nails, and put my hand into His side, I will not believe." Thomas doubted, Thomas did not believe. All unbelief is unreasonable, stubborn, self-willed boastful, and deceitful. Thomas said, "Jesus is going to have to prove to me that He has risen from the grave."

How many of us have said, "Jesus, you have to prove to me that you are real and alive." God will prove Himself to you, as Jesus did to Thomas.

The next Sunday after the resurrection, Thomas went to Church, as we would say it today. Again Christ appeared with them and gave the usual salutation, "Peace be unto you." The doors were again shut, emphasizing again that the resurrected body can go through material substance without an opening. He simply

197

appeared, in their presence, as on the other occasion. After teaching them He vanished out of their sight.

But after appearing, this day, and Thomas was there, Jesus said, "Thomas, reach hither your finger, and behold my hand, and thrust it into My side, and be not faithless, but believing." And Thomas answered and said unto Jesus, "My Lord and my God."

Thomas was not with the first gathering of Christians, but when He heard that they had seen Jesus alive and that He had appeared to them on the first Sunday, he was determined to be present on the next Sunday when they were gathered again. Jesus as usual, satisfied the doubting and unbelief of Thomas.

Thomas said, "My Lord and my God." This is not a mere exclamation, but one of the plainest and most irresistible testimonies of the deity of Jesus Christ. Whether he did feel the nail prints and the spear wound in His side is not stated in scripture. Thomas was the first to give the title of God to Jesus, other that the prophets in predicting these events.

Jesus said, "Because you Thomas, has seen Me, you have believed, blessed are they that have not seen, and yet have believed." No special blessing is pronounced on those who have seen God over those who have not seen Him.

Other signs Jesus did in the presence of His disciples led John to write, "I did not write in this book; but I have written these things, that you might believe that Jesus is the Christ, the Son of God; and that believing you might have life through His Name."

John says I write this to you, "To prove beyond all doubt, that

Jesus of Nazareth is the promised Messiah and God's Son, and that we might have full redemption and benefits of the Gospel by faith."

Have you read John's Gospel that was inspired by God Himself? Have you studied God's Word? Have you let the Holy Spirit teach you God's Word?

John said, "I wrote this for only one purpose, and that is that you might know for sure that Jesus is the Christ, the Son of God; and that you might have eternal life with Jesus, your Lord, forever." Amen.

Obligated-Eager-Proud
Romans 1:14-25

Paul said, he is obligated and he said, "I am under obligation or bound to tell everyone about Jesus." Paul says in Romans 8:12, "Brethren (fellow Christians) we are debtor, not to the flesh, not to live after the flesh. For if you live after the flesh, you shall die; but if you through the spirit do mortify the deeds of the body, you shall live. For as many as are led by the spirit of God, they are the sons of God. The Spirit itself bears witness with our spirit, that we are the children of God."

We owe the flesh nothing. It has no more control of our lives. We must not live in the sins of the flesh or we shall die, but if we will put to death the practices of the flesh by the spirit we shall live. You have not received a spirit of slavery to relapse again into fear and terror, but you have received the spirit of freedom and son-ship, to break every bond to the devil. You will know in your spirit, that you are the sons of God.

Our spirits have been made partakers of their spiritual things; their duty is also to minister to them in earthly things. We should come in the fullness of the blessings of the gospel of Jesus Christ. We are obligated to all who know and to all who do not know Christ, whether they be Jew or Gentile, saved or unsaved, wise or stupid. We are obligated the same as Paul was, because we too are the son's of God as he is.

Paul goes on to say, "I am eager to preach the gospel to you." I am ready Paul says, I am ready, willing, and able. Ready because He had prepared himself. Ready because God had prepared him. Ready because he now knew for sure that Jesus was what He said He was.

He was willing because he believed God and His Word. Willing because he knew the Word to be true. Willing because he knew the difference it had made in his life.

I am able because God's Son Jesus Himself sent me. I am able because I too, have been baptized with the Holy Spirit. I am able because I know that what I teach is true.

And further more Paul says, "I am not ashamed" of the Gospel of Jesus Christ, for it is the power of God to salvation, to everyone that believes. I am proud of the gospel. I am proud to receive the power of God. I am not proud of my past, but I am proud of my present status, and I know my future.

It is in God's power to:
1. Produce the new birth.
2. Give salvation.
3. Impart grace.
4. Establish the faith.
5. Generate faith.

6. Set free.
7. Nourish Spiritual life.
8. Cleanse the church.
9. Impart immortality.
10. Bring peace.
11. Give protection.
12. Give fullness of blessings.

All this He is in His power to everyone that believes in Him. Do you believe in your heart?

God's righteousness is revealed in the Gospel on the ground of faith, as the absolute condition of salvation, and is only effective in those who believe.

The just must live by continued faith, and go from faith to faith as light is received.

Paul goes on to say, "But the wrath of God is also revealed in the gospel as part of God's righteousness." Why? Because that which may be known of God is made manifest in them, for God has showed it unto them.

Paul explains this by saying that all invisible things, even the eternal power and Godhead, are clearly seen by the visible things of creation. God is revealed by the things He created, so Paul is saying there is no excuse for men to be ignorant of invisible things. So man is without excuse. When they knew God (knew God by experience), they even then didn't glorify Him as God, nor were they thankful. They made God a mystery and gave the people images of all kind.

202

GRANDPA'S LESSONS ABOUT JESUS

Are we guilty of making God the Father, Jesus the Son, and the Holy Spirit a mystery to our fellow man? Jesus came to solve this mystery. Images of men, birds, cattle, dogs, frogs, snakes are common among idol worshippers. When they formed their gods in human shape, they showed them with passion and represented them as disgraceful sex perversions. They were sex gods.

So God also gave them up to their sins, and permitted them to dishonor their own bodies between themselves, to homosexual sins. Why? Because they changed the truth of God into a lie, and worshipped and served the creature more than the Creator, who is blessed forever…Amen. God saw they had an evil, faithless mind, and gave them over to it.

Be alert and examine the visible things that God created and you will see God in all of it. You will see the invisible things of God.

Paul wrote these things to you and preached these truths, while here on earth, because he said and knew that he was obligated, to do so. Not only obligated, but being obligated Paul was eager to spread the truth about Jesus. Going forth teaching Jesus, Paul said, "I am proud." Now you go forth feeling obligated, eager and proud to be a witness for Jesus. Hold your head high and go forth telling others, not only telling but more important, go forth living it as Paul did.

What We Do or What We Say
1 Corinthians Chapter 2

Paul said: "When I came to you, I came not with excellent speech or of wisdom; but I came declaring to you the testimony of God. When I came to you, I was determined not to teach any other teaching, except the teaching of Jesus Christ and the benefits of the cross.

"The virgin birth makes the difference. The cross and Christ crucified makes the difference. The resurrection makes the difference.

"I was with you in weakness, fear, and trembling. I came not on My own strength; but on the strength given me by God Himself. I totally depend upon God.

"My speech and my preaching came not from words of man; but in demonstration of the Spirit and of power given me by the Spirit. I used none of the means of great orators to sway men. I preached under the anointing and the power of the spirit and confirmed what I preached with signs following. I used this method so that your faith might be in the power of God, not of human wisdom.

"The wisdom of God, the gospel of Jesus Christ, which was hidden up to the time of its revelation and which God ordained before this age for us. None of the rulers of this world knew this revelation. If they had known it they would not have crucified the Lord."

Prophets searched diligently to understand what they taught about it, and even angels themselves desired to comprehend it. Such mystery is now made clear through the preaching of the apostles, and the revelations of the scriptures of the New Testament.

God had pre-determined; God simply determined to bring about His plan for the food of all who ever would believe.

Paul says that, "Spiritual things, are Spirit revealed and taught. Eyes has not seen, nor ear heard, neither have entered into the heart of man, the things which God has prepared for them that love Him." (1 Corinthians 2:9)

But God has revealed them unto us by His Spirit. For your spirit, Paul says, is always searching the deep things of God.

Paul names three different spirits here:
1. The Spirit of God. (1 Cor 2:11)
2. The spirit of man. (1 Cor 2:11)
3. The spirit of the World. (1 Cor 2:12)

But now we have the spirit of God, since we have received

Christ, not the spirit of the world that we might know the things that are freely given to us of God.

Two kinds of wisdom: (1 Cor 2:13)
1. Words of man's wisdom
2. Words of Holy Spirit's wisdom.

The natural man receives not the things of the Spirit of God, for they are foolishness to him. Neither can he know them, because they are spiritually discerned. This is man living under the control of the flesh's passions, the depraved part of man in contrast with the rational part. He is an animal man as opposed to the spiritual man. He has no sense of spiritual values and no relish for them. He counts it the highest wisdom to live for this world and carnal pleasures. He cannot see their supreme excellence due to animal appetites and be spiritually dead.

The spiritual man, this man is living under the control of the Holy Spirit and minds the things of the spirit. He has the mind of Christ and discerns and recognizes spiritual things above the worldly things. He is a new creature and resurrected from death in trespasses and sins. The lower animal passions have been crucified and put off.

But he that is spiritual examines, convinces, and reproves the natural man of his evil ways, yet no one is able to find fault with the Godly man.

Who of the natural men that live in the worldly passions can know the mind of the Lord that he may instruct the spiritual man?

GRANDPA'S LESSONS ABOUT JESUS

In Matthew 15:10-11, Jesus called the multitude and said unto them, "Hear and understand, not that which goes into the mouth defiles a man, but that which comes out of the mouth, this defiles a man." Jesus said, those things that proceed out of the mouth, come forth out of the heart; and they defile the man. For out of the heart proceed evil thoughts, murders, adulteries, fornications, thefts, false witness, etc. These are the things that defile a man.

Paul says the Word must be in your mouth and in your heart, that is the Word of faith, which we preach.

Jesus said, "Why do you call me Lord, Lord, and not do the things I tell you?"

Jesus said in Matthew 7:21: "Not everyone that says to me, Lord, Lord shall enter into the kingdom of Heaven; but he that does the will of My Father which is in Heaven. Many will say to Me, in that day, Lord, Lord, have we not prophesied in Your Name? And In Your Name have we not cast out devils? And in Your Name done many wonderful works? And then will I profess unto them, I never knew you. Depart from Me, you that work iniquity."

I looked up to church people when I was a child. My idols were church people. One day I saw a neighbor go into a house of prostitution. Another time I saw another church person drink whiskey while working on a tractor. These things broke my heart, but thank God I saw my friend as a Sunday school superintendent, another as a janitor and one as a Sunday school teacher. These turned out to be my real heroes I looked up to. They all professed to be followers of Christ, but they did not all walk what they talked.

Some one is looking at you today. Are they going to be proud of you? Are you going to disappoint them, break their heart by what you are doing, or by what you are saying?

Are you living what you are saying? Is your man spirit dwelling with the spirit of the world or with the Spirit of God?

The Way of Salvation
Luke 18:10-14

It makes all the difference in the way we approach the Lord, or the attitude in which we come to Him.

The Pharisees were strict, ambitious, educated, patriotic, zealous, prayerful, and concerning the Law, blameless. They believed in Angels, spirits, miracles, and the resurrection. They fasted, paid their tithes, and attended church. They respected their ministers and their church. In fact they were what people called the holiness group in their day.

We have no proof that this man, who went up to the temple to pray, was being dishonest. Like the rich young ruler, he had better testimony than many of us today.

However, the Pharisees invariably depended upon their own righteousness. It seemed that they were not conscious of this many times.

Learn from this scripture, that our righteousness will not

purchase salvation. Notice that in that one prayer the Pharisee used the pronoun "I" five times, while the Publican left this "I" out altogether.

The Publican was really depending on the merits of the Lord instead of His own merits. He was really saying, "Lord, be merciful unto me a sinner," showing that he believed in the atonement.

Look at the two thieves on the cross. One confessed his sins, trusting in the debt, which Jesus was paying, while the other considered himself as good as Jesus, justifying himself. The one who relied on the righteousness of Jesus, rather than his own righteousness, was at that moment justified, "just as if he had never sinned" in God's sight.

I read a story once about two lawyers who stopped at a revival meeting. Both of them became convicted and went to the altar. One was saved and other was not. One said to the other, "tell me how you were saved. I pled my case and pled my case and I didn't get anything." "That is where you missed it," answered the other. "You should have plead guilty and you would have gotten somewhere."

Saul and David both sinned. Saul went on depending on who he was, while David confessed, "I am the Man." David was a man after God's own heart. Saul died in his sins.

Peter and Judas both sinned. Peter wept the bitter tears of true repentance. Judas came back, but in the wrong attitude and went down.

GRANDPA'S LESSONS ABOUT JESUS

I appreciate good moral people. There are good men and women. By this I mean they are true to their word. I know some good moral men that I can trust more than I could some religious people. They are good enough that I would be willing to loan them my last dollar, because I know they would repay. But their goodness is not enough to save them. A man cannot lift him self up by his own boot straps. We must have the Savior. Our righteousness is as filthy rags if we trust it to save us. All have sinned and come short of the glory of God. As valuable as you might believe your works are, as good as they might be, your works will not even pay the interest on the soul; it is so valuable.

If a sinner trusts in anything else, other than the Blood of Jesus, he is doomed. The wrath of God abides on him. (John 3:36) If he comes up any other way he is a thief and a robber (John 10). Without the shedding of blood there is no remission for sins. All other belief is false.

The death angel took all who did not have the blood over the doorpost. Jesus is the passover Lamb. He is the Door. There is no other name given among men whereby we may be saved. If we do not believe in the Son we are anti-Christ. (1 John 4:3)

Church membership will not save you. A good name will never save you. Being a good citizen will never save you. Only the shed blood of Jesus saves. We may confess our sins of our wife, our husband, our dad, our mother. We may confess the sins of our community, school,church or organization; but if we confess our sins, He is faithful and just to forgive our sins and cleanse us from all unrighteousness.

Many come to seek Christ thinking surely they can be saved

211

easily because they believe in a holiness church. A denominational church, a main line church. Some think it will be easy for them to be saved because their parents were good people; because they are prominent citizens, good business men and women or have a good reputation. That is the wrong attitude. I've had people tell me that I should quit praying for some people; because some other people better thought of and I should pray for them first. That is the wrong attitude.
One must know that he is lost before he may be saved. He must confess that to God. You will never be saved until you are first unsaved. When you give up, God begins.

You can never save a drowning person until they stop trying to save their self, and puts his trust in you. You can never save a sinner until he stops trying to save himself through his own righteousness.

One day Jesus went home with a church member named Simon, the Pharisee. Just before they ate dinner a girl was passing by, and the very presence of Jesus caused this poor fallen girl to become convicted of her sins. She began to shed tears. Then she caught herself doing an unheard of thing. She was in the house washing the feet of Jesus with her tears, and drying them with her long hair. Simon did not like this at all. He felt that this had disgraced his home. He detested such low class women.

He said if Jesus had known what a low class woman that was, he would not have allowed her to touch Him. Jesus knew what she had been, and He knew who she was now. For she had been translated into the family of God. Although Simon did not understand it, the grace of God had set her free, and made her "just a if she had never sinned," justified in God's sight. He probably thought she could not be saved unless she was put under the water and joined his church, but I believe her sins were forgiven right that second. Because Jesus said, "Woman, your sins, which are many are forgiven you."

Did you ever have Jesus say that to you? You can if you will come pleading the righteousness and goodness of Jesus instead of your own goodness. Trust in what He has done, instead of what you have done. He has paid for your sins. All you need to do is to confess Him as your savior and live for Him and obey Him.

Now back to the scripture that we started with. First the Publican did not pray to be heard of men. He prayed a short prayer. Next he was convicted, he had true repentance. He had burden. He had a load. He was conscious of it as he smote upon his breast. Next he confessed his sins and asked for mercy. Next he went home justified.

I can just see that Publican now. His face sad and long, and after he prayed, I can see a cloud of conviction settle over his face. I can see true repentance grip him as the tears slowly started down his face. I can see his face lighting up. I can tell his load is lifted. His hands go up into the air. He cries a little. He laughs a little. Then I am sure he shouted a little.

Our righteousness will never purchase us salvation. Trust in what Jesus has done for you instead of what you have done.

For with the heart man believes unto righteousness and with the mouth confession is made unto salvation. (Romans 10:10)

Commands For Christians
Ephesians 5:6-21

Let no man deceive you with vain words (verse 6), because of these things comes the wrath of God upon the children of disobedience. Be not therefore partakers with them.

Do not listen to those that teach customs, rituals or words that are not God's Words, ways that are not God's way. For if you believe other than the Word of God you shall not inherit God's Kingdom.

Paul says for you were sometimes in darkness, but now you are light in the Lord, so walk as children of light.

We were all at one time children of darkness. By this Paul means that we were all walking in sin before we accepted Christ as our Lord and Saviour. We should not have fellowship with the unfruitful works of darkness, but rather we should express disapproval of these works. It does not say we should not have fellowship with the person; but it says we should not have fellowship with the works of Satan.

214

GRANDPA'S LESSONS ABOUT JESUS

It is a shame, even to speak of those things that take place in darkness. When you keep talking of the things of Satan, it brings attention to Satan instead of God and Jesus Christ. Jesus brings all these things done in darkness to light. Jesus sees all in darkness and light.

Paul says, "Christian awaken, you that sleep, arise from the dead and Christ shall give you light." See that you walk cautiously, not as fools, but as wise, redeeming the time, because the days are evil. Awake, and walk about watching on every hand to avoid danger and enemies. Live the Gospel by watching your conduct.

How often we try to hide behind God's misquoted Word? How often we try to hide behind sin? How often we try to hide in darkness? We think this is the answer because we can't face facts, but this is not the answer, Paul says.

Sleep does not make our troubles and problems disappear. Alcohol and drugs do not make our problems disappear. Hiding in darkness does not make our problems disappear. Paul said, "Awake, my friends arise, do not play dead, come to Christ and he will give you life. He will give you light. Do not be a fool and throw your life away. Watch on every hand to avoid danger and enemies." Live by the Gospels. Paul says, "Let me give you some good advice. Redeem the time, because the days are evil."

"Buy every moment which others throw away. Improve every moment to make up for those lost in sin." How much we have to make up, how many moments we have wasted and thrown away. Time cannot be put in a bank and drawn out as we want or as we have need of them. When time is gone it is gone. Wake up, Paul says, improve every moment to make up for those you lost in sin.

Paul said, "Be not unwise, but understanding what the will of the Lord is." Did you hear this? Don't be senseless, crazed. Don't become mad men. Be sober, be decent, modest and be Christ like.

Be not filled with wine in excess, but be filled with the Holy Spirit. Some religions pushed drunkenness and sex orgies of immoral acts. Paul says sin in drinking in excess and drugs make you do things you wouldn't do otherwise.

Instead, be filled with the Holy Spirit. This is the privilege of every Christian. It is true that every born-again man receives the spirit of sonship and has the Holy Spirit in a measure, but this is not the kind of filling one may yet receive if he will accept truth and seek God for the fullness of the Spirit; the Holy Spirit without measure.

Verses 19-20 tell us other things we should do as Christians. Read Psalms, sing hymns and spiritual songs, making melody in your hearts. Giving thanks always for all things unto God and the Father in the Name of our Lord Jesus Christ.

Do these things because of continued blessings from God. Through Jesus Christ alone, we can approach God, in the Name of Jesus Christ. Only by the authority of Jesus Christ can we do these things.

Let no man be stubborn in his opinion to disturb the peace of the church. Submitting your selves one to another in the fear of God and the reverence of God.

Not I, but the Father. Thank you, Father.

Pentecost

What really happened at Pentecost? What really happened at Jerusalem? (John 14:15-17,26, Acts 1:4-5, 8-9, Acts 2:1-8, 11-15, 22-24, 32-47)

Pentecost took place fifty days after the resurrection of Jesus Christ our Lord.

All of the 120 were of one mind. None were uninterested, unconcerned. None were lukewarm; but all were earnest and united in faith and prayer. They were there looking, expecting something. Why were you at church last Sunday? They were probably in the temple court, where they had met regularly for prayer and not in the upper room where they had residence during this time.

The Holy Spirit filled the house and moved upon the 120 flowing out of their innermost beings like rivers of living waters, pouring abundantly like a mighty stream, full of power from on high. It was like a mighty rushing wind, or the blast of a clap of thunder sweeping before it.

They were both filled and baptized with the Spirit. Saints had many experiences and blessings in times ahead of Pentecost. They were filled and had the spirit in them. The Holy Spirit came within, into, upon and they were moved by it. But none were baptized in the Spirit. John the Baptist was filled with the spirit, but he was not baptized. Mary was filled about 35 years before she was baptized with the spirit at Pentecost. Jesus was filled about 30 years before He was baptized with the spirit. The disciples were filled and had the spirit in them 3 years before they were baptized with the spirit. Old Testament saints had gifts and fruits of the spirit, in different measures of the spirit, but not the spirit baptism or the spirit without measure.

The disciples had gifts and great powers years before the spirit baptism. The disciples were told to get the spirit baptism, before starting their ministry. This was a command from Jesus.

Old Testament saints and the disciples had many blessings:
1. Salvation.
2. Redemption.
3. Healing.
4. Names written in Heaven.
5. The new birth.
6. Conversion.
7. Righteousness.
8. Justification.
9. Holiness
10. Pure hearts.
11. Sanctification.
12. And many other blessings...

GRANDPA'S LESSONS ABOUT JESUS

They were saved and were God's children and Heaven bound. Therefore, one should not take any of these blessings as evidence of a spirit baptism. From all of this we gather that the spirit baptism is the fullness of God in the lives of believers, not the spirit by measure as in the Old Testament times, but the spirit without measure.

The difference between a filling and a baptism, or the spirit by measure, and the spirit without measure, may be illustrated by a glass and a pitcher of water, to the extent the water is poured into the glass it is filled, but not baptized. By burying the glass in the fullness of the water it is both filled and baptized.

Taking the glass out of the fullness of the water it is no longer baptized. So it is with believers, to the extent that one is filled with the spirit he has that measure of power and can do things according to the degree of anointing he has. If he is merely filled by the spirit by measure, he is limited in spiritual power, and if he has the spirit in all fullness here is no limitation. He can do the works of Christ and the Apostles.

A filling always comes with a baptism, but a baptism does not always come with a filling. At Pentecost they were both filled and baptized, and many fillings kept coming to them to replenish the spirit and power they had received. One must continue to live and walk in the Spirit and be filled with all the fullness of God in order to maintain fullness of the baptism.

The Spirit spoke through the disciples, to all whom were present that they might hear in their own language. Please remember the speaking of tongues we have it today is a very touchy subject. This is the way it should be. We must be sure that what we speak

220

is under direct inspiration of the Holy Spirit and not the person exercising the gift by himself.

The noise of the clap of thunder and of the rushing wind must have alarmed the whole city and they came running to the temple where they found the disciples full of the spirit and speaking in all languages. They said, "What is going on here these men must be drunk."

But Peter said, "It is only 9 a.m. No Jews drink this time of the day even an alcoholic does not."

The speaking of tongues ended and Peter began speaking in his own language, which all 16 different nations could understand. Peter said, "What you have just witnessed, is a fulfilling of prophecy."

Now in verse 21 of Acts chapter 2 reads, "And it shall come to pass, that whosoever shall call upon the Name of the Lord shall be saved." This will be true as long as there are sinners to repent. There is no such doctrine in scripture as the door of mercy being closed to Jews or Gentiles at any time, before their death.

Now Peter goes on telling about the Christ, He said, "In the foreknowledge of God, He saw it was necessary for Him to send a Savior for men or His eternal program with them would come to naught. God determined and planned a sacrifice to save men and permitted the wicked hands of men to slay it."

But God loosed Christ from the bonds of death, which had no more claim on Him when He paid the debt for man and conquered death.

The souls and spirits of men are immortal and never go to the grave. The body only goes there for it is the only part of man that is made of dust.

Before Christ all souls (minds) and spirits went to a place called Sheol or Hades once, being held in separate compartments. Christ rescued righteous souls and spirits out of hell and took them to Heaven with Him when He ascended on High. Now a saved soul and spirit goes to Heaven at death. The wicked ones continue to go to hell until the resurrection.

Christ's body did not see corruption, but was raised from the dead as an eternal, immortal flesh and bone body, not as a spiritual being.

Take notice of verse 37: "This pricked their hearts and they said, 'What shall we do?' Then Peter said repent, and be baptized every one of you in the Name of Jesus Christ, for the remission of sins, and you shall receive the gift of the Holy Spirit." In the Name of Jesus means, "being baptized by the authority of Jesus Christ." Repent before baptism, and then one is a fit candidate for water baptism, which is an outward symbol of the death, burial, and resurrection of Jesus Christ. It testifies to the world that one has already repented and been forgiven by faith in Christ Jesus.

After this repenting and water baptism, we have the promise that if and when one repents and his sins are forgiven, he can have the Spirit baptism for the promise is to all men in verse 39.

On the same day 3000 souls were baptized, and the disciples continued in the teaching of Jesus by:

222

GRANDPA'S LESSONS ABOUT JESUS

1. Teaching the doctrine of Christ.
2. Having fellowship.
3. Praising, worshipping, and witnessing.
4. Having Holy Communion.
5. Praying.

Fear came upon Jerusalem, for several weeks past they had seen great miracles and were seeing them daily, and so there was fear upon the people. They continued praising God for daily those who were hearing and obeying the Word of God as it was preached to the people, and the Lord added to His Church daily those that were saved.

They came looking, expecting. Why did you come to church today?

These people were saved, had salvation, but wanted *more*. They were filled, but limited in the spirit. They wanted the promise of Jesus, spirit without measure.

They came looking, expecting, believing, and doing so, Jesus kept His promise. They received, and now were able to continue the work exactly as Jesus did, when He walked the earth. But once this baptism is received we must continue to live and walk in the spirit, if we are to continue in this baptism.

This is the time to take a minute to remember. Remember you do not go to the grave, only your body does. You are not a body with a mind and a spirit; but you are a spirit with a mind and a body. So if your parents, children, friends were saved, and when you go to the cemetery the next time don't be sad, for they (the spirit) is in Heaven with God, if they had repented and believed and accepted Jesus as their Lord and Savior. On the other hand if they were lost, if they had not repented and accepted Jesus as their Lord and Savior, I am afraid they (their spirit) are in Hell awaiting judgment.

Forgiveness
Psalms 32

Blessed is he whose transgression is forgiven, whose sin is covered. When we repent, our sins are forgiven. When we are forgiven, our sins are covered. Our sins are destroyed. When we are forgiven we are covered with the Blood of Jesus. When we are forgiven, our sins are not held against us any longer. When we are forgiven, our spirit is cleansed of all guile.

Jesus says, "Forgive your people who have sinned." I have sinned. You have sinned. I was dirty and you were dirty. I hated myself when I sinned against God. I repented and Jesus forgave me my sins. Jesus was merciful unto me and He healed my soul. God will forgive us our sins, for if we also forgive every one that is indebted to us. It says in the Lords prayer, "Forgive us our trespasses as we forgive those that trespass against us." The Publican said, "Lord be merciful to me a sinner, and he went down to his house justified." (Just as if he had never sinned.)

Once our sins are covered, they are pardoned. The forgiving is done by God when one confesses his sins, and exercises his faith in the atoning blood of Jesus Christ. Confess to God.

David said, "When I kept silent about my sins, and held them inside of me, my bones waxed old. God your hand was heavy upon me, because of my sins. My moisture is turned into the drought of summer." Did you ever notice how dry you feel when you sin?

David said he acknowledged his sin to God. He didn't hide it from God, but he said he would confess his sins unto the Lord and He forgave him his sin. Praise the Lord. So David says to pray to the Lord while He may be found. (2 Cor 6:2.) Paul says, "For he said, I have heard you in a time accepted, and in the day of salvation have I sought you in time of need; behold, now is the accepted time. Behold, now is the day of salvation. Many sorrows shall be to those who will not confess and be forgiven; but he that trust in the Lord, mercy shall surround him."

So be glad in the Lord, and rejoice, you righteous; and shout for joy, all you that are upright in heart.

In John 8:7-11 the woman had committed adultery. Jesus said, "He that is without sin among you, let him first cast a stone at her." And the men that heard it, being convicted by their own sin, went out one by one, and the woman was left alone. Jesus then asked, "Woman, where are those your accusers? Has no man condemned you?" She said, "No Lord." Jesus said, "Neither do I condemn you, go and sin no more." He said you are forgiven. Praise the Lord.

Jesus did not condone the sin of adultery, but He simply forgave the woman, as He had done others who were sinful. He frankly told her to sin no more, proving He did condemn adultery as a sin, but He forgave her.

John wrote: "If we confess our sins, He is faithful and just to forgive us our sins, and to cleanse us from all unrighteousness…I write unto you, little children, because your sins are forgiven you for His Name's sake, or through the name of Jesus." The man with palsy was let down through the roof. Jesus saw their faith, and He said unto him, "Man your sins are forgiven you."

Luke writes in Acts 13:38, "Be it known unto, you therefore men and brethren, that through Jesus Christ, and faith in Him, through this man is preached unto you the forgiveness of sins. And all that believe are justified from all things, from which you could not be justified by the laws of Moses."

Jesus appeared to Paul on the road to Damascus. Jesus said, "I am Jesus, who you persecute. I am sending you to open the eyes of the Gentiles and to turn them from darkness to light. And from the power of Satan unto God, that they may receive forgiveness of sins, and inheritance among them which are sanctified by faith that is in me."

1 Colossians 1:12-14 Paul writes, "Give thanks to the Father who has delivered us from the power of darkness, and has translated us into the Kingdom of His dear Son, in whom we have redemption through His blood, even the forgiveness of sins."

He says God wants to transfer you from Satan and his power and kingdom of sin to be placed under the government of the

Son of God's love. The transfer is made possible by redemption through the blood of Christ.

Paul writes to the Romans in 2:1-2, "Therefore you are inexcusable, O man, whosoever you are that judges, for where in you judge another, you condemn yourself, for you that judges do the same things." But we are sure that the judgment of God is according to truth against them, which commit such things.

Some justify themselves and condemn others. They are guilty of some of the same things God condemns others for.

John 3:17, "For God sent not His Son into the world to condemn the world, but that the world through Him might be saved."

The lame man laid by the pool for 38 years, waiting on the troubled waters. Jesus said, "Wilt you be made whole? Rise take up your bed and walk." Immediately He walked. Jesus said, "Behold you are made whole, sin no more, lest a worse thing come unto you."

Romans 3:23, "For all have sinned, and come short of the glory of God."

Romans 6:23, "For the wage of sin is death, but the gift of God is eternal life through Jesus Christ our Lord."

Acts 16:30-31, "And brought them out, and said, sirs, what must I do to be saved? And they said, believe on the Lord Jesus Christ, and you will be saved, and your house."

Romans 10:9, "If you shall confess with your mouth the Lord Jesus, and shall believe in your heart that God has raised him from the dead, you shall be saved. For with the heart man believes unto righteousness, and with the mouth confession is made unto salvation. For the scripture says, whosoever believes on Him shall not be ashamed, for there is no difference between the Jew and the Greek. The same Lord over all is rich unto all that call upon Him. For whosoever shall call upon the Name of Lord shall be saved."

Lord, be merciful unto me a sinner.

John 3:16, "For God so loved the world that He gave His only begotten Son that whosoever believes in Him should not perish, but have everlasting life."

Matt 5:16, "Let your light so shine before men, that they may see your good works, and glorify your Father which is in Heaven."

"For what is man's advantage if he gain the whole world, and lose his self, or be cast away?" (Luke 9:25)

1 John 1:10, "If we say that we have not sinned, we make Him a liar, and His Word is not in us."

Isaiah 43:25, "I, even I, am He that blots out your transgressions for mine own sake, and will not remember your sins."

Sinners do not deserve forgiveness or any claim to such blessing. They deserve full punishment, but God undertakes, by free grace, the pardon of all sin, which is repented of, and cancellation of punishment for rebellion. He can, for God's sake that men are forgiven and they escape hell. Thereby, they owe their lives to him to live for His glory, and not to live unto themselves. If men are to be pardoned, they must come, not to justify themselves, but to confess their sins so that He can be glorified. Unless they come on His terms they can never be forgiven.

We have an important road to travel ahead in going forth for God, in building His Church.

We have a lot of praying to do, 24 hours a day. We must put our complete trust, our complete faith in God. We must cleanse our churches. We must be clean as we stand before God. We must cleanse ourselves.

God said as I read to you, "I am He that blots out your transgressions for mine own sake, and will not remember your sins." God wants the church for Himself, not just for us. He wants a church in the community He can use to save souls. "I am He that blots out your transgressions. I am He that cleans you up." We must make sure we stand clean before God will you let Him cleanse you today?

What The Bible Has To Say About Hell
Luke 16:19-31

The liberal preacher tells us that our God is a God of love; therefore, He would not send anyone to burn in the flames of hell for eternity.

Others, perhaps you, believe that hell exists with your head, but down in your heart you doubt. If someone stopped you on the street and asked you if you never witness for Christ, you never really pray for the unsaved, you never weep over your lost loved ones.

So our society today, as a whole, does not believe in hell. The Bible, which is filled with the subject of hell, is largely ignored. Let's see what the Bible has to say about hell.

Luke 16:19-31
First of all the Bible proves that there is life after death. Notice if you will in verse 22, "And it came to pass, the beggar died, and was carried by the angels into the bosom of Abraham. The rich man also died, and was buried."

Now they both died. It doesn't matter if the man is rich or poor. It doesn't matter if the man is popular or unpopular. The Bible says that the men die. The Bible says, "It is appointed unto men once to die, but after this the judgment."

The Bible says you are going to die. God wants you to understand that it's appointed unto men once to die, but after this the judgment. And so the beggar died, and the rich man died. Every 100 years a complete new generation comes upon the face of the earth. Men die. God wants you to know this. So there is a life after death. Men all through the ages have tried somehow to do away with facing the fact that every body dies.

Now think about it. Here was Lazarus. Can you see him in your mind? He was laid every day at the gate of the rich man's home. I can see him as he lies there in his old rags, probably with leprosy. The Bible says, "Moreover the dogs came and licked his sores." And I can see the rich man as he passed by everyday clothed in purple and fine linen, very best of everything. He walked by and said, "Well, good morning, Lazarus."

Lazarus would look up at him and no doubt say, "Well you had better put your faith and trust in God."

Then, you can hear the rich man reply, "Well I am a member of this big church downtown. I'm a member of this lodge and that one and it's all right, Lazarus, for poor fools like you to believe in the Supreme Being, and in heaven and hell, but we've got an educated preacher. Why, he's just fresh out of seminary, and he's giving us the right thing. Its all right, Lazarus."

He said, to the guard, "Bring him a little extra crumbs today."

"You got a God, Lazarus? Well, why are you eating crumbs?" He said, "They've got a big t-bone steak ready for me in there."

I can see somebody as one day they walked into the house and said to the rich man. "You remember old Lazarus, don't you? Well, we found him out there this morning, dead and cold." The rich man said, "Oh, that is a shame. Poor old man, he believed some how there was a God somewhere and that some day he would go and live in Heaven. He kept telling me about hell. Well, it's just pitiful." He said, "Well, call the garbage man."

They came and picked him up that old cold, dead body and as they looked at the rags, one of them said, "I have seen this old boy many times. I didn't know he was in such bad shape. Why, he's just skin and bones. Had I known that, I would have brought a little something for him myself." They put the body in the back of the wagon and took it over to the valley of Gehenna, where they burn the refuse and trash. They took the body of Lazarus and said, "One, two, and the third time threw it on the trash heap and it burned."

They said he died but they never moved old Lazarus. They moved his body, but "to be absent from the body is to be present with the Lord." And before they ever discovered he was dead, angels had gathered up his soul and spirit and he was in the bosom of Abraham.

Not long after that the doctors were hurrying back and forth into the rich man's mansion. Finally one of them said, "Well, it looks like a heart attack." The other agreed. Whatever it might have been, the rich man died. I imagine they called the morticians and they got him ready, and the mourning went on for several days.

But the rich man died and was buried. The Bible did not say that the poor man was buried. But it said this rich man was buried. And while the preacher was saying, "We've got every reason to believe that he is in heaven tonight." The bible says, "He lifted up his eyes and began to scream, I'm tormented in these flames."

My friends God wants you to know there is something on the other side, on the other side of the grave. Your life doesn't stop at the grave. You had better believe it.

First of all, God wants you to see that you are going to die.

Second, God wants you to know that there is life after death. The Bible teaches us and the Bible proves that death does not end it all. Death does not end it all. Death is just a beginning point. Death is just opening a door and walking you through to a new life and new world. God didn't create us to die. God created us to live forever. Every one of you is going to live forever in Heaven or hell. You are going to live in one of the two places. The rich man did and Lazarus did and so has everyone who has ever died. From this community, from the face of the earth, they are living somewhere today in either Heaven or hell.

Some people tell me they would like to end it all. To these people I say, "There is your mistake, you can't end it all, and Lazarus didn't end it all, they lived on."

We look through the cemetery where you loved ones are buried, but praise God they are not there. The Bible says they're in heaven. Paul said, "Absent from the body, present with the Lord." The Bible says, "Even so we also which sleep in Jesus will God bring with him."

Jesus said, "I am the resurrection and the life; he that believes in Me shall never die." Do you believe this?

Speaking of the soul and spirit, he says here, Lazarus was still living, although the body was dead, and the rich man was living long after his body was buried. So it does away with the theory of soul sleep.

If God would make himself visible and walk back and forth and look at you he could say, "You're saved," or "You are not saved." God knows where you live and God knows everything about you and God knows tonight whether you are saved or lost. God looks at this congregation and He sees two kinds of people. He sees the saved and the lost people. That is all there is. There is no middle division. There is no middle of the road. There is no way out. You are either completely saved or you are completely lost.

Hell actually exists. The Bible proves it. You know the first hell-fire and damnation preacher? He told the Scribes and the Pharisees, "Oh, you hypocrites, on the outside you look like a sepulcher while on the inside you are full of uncleanness and dead men's bones. You are in danger of fire and damnation." We need to keep it in mind what Jesus said.

We hear some modern preachers today say, "God's too merciful to send one of His children to hell." Well, He is exactly right. Praise God, I believe that too. The thing that you need to understand is, until you are saved, you're not a child of God. The Bible says in John 8:44, "You are of your Father the devil." God never will send His children to hell, thank God for that. Isn't that wonderful?

I don't want to go to hell. I thank God I'm not going. When I study about this and when I read about it, and when I have to preach on it, I don't know anything that draws me closer to Jesus Christ. I don't want to go to hell.

Let me ask you something. Will you explain to me why it is, if there is no hell, why this Book tells more about it than most any other subject in the Bible?

Why is it the churches who believes in hell are the soul winning churches across America? You will see big churches that don't believe it, but they're not soul winning churches. They get big because they are social gathering places. The churches that believe that there is a hell are soul-winning churches, and God expects them to become the great churches across America. They are still, the salt of the earth and if it wasn't for them I wonder what would happen to America. Why is it that men will forsake their families, and forsake fortunes, many times a fine position, to go out and warn people that there is a hell?

The Bible proves that there is no hope of a second chance. There is a second chance on this side, but there is none on the other side. There is a great gulf fixed.

The Bible proves there will be recognition beyond the grave. Do you hear what this man is saying? "Send Lazarus that he might testify to my brethren lest they come to this awful place." Have you ever thought about it? Do you think that rich man would have sent Lazarus to his brother's house while he was alive? No. He would have died before he would have Lazarus to witness to his brother, but when he got into hell he looked around and probably saw some of the fellows who had tried to lead him astray with their false doctrine. He might have seen some of the preachers that he had seen running off to these awful places and said, "I don't want them to go to my brother." He said, "Abraham would you send Lazarus? Send Lazarus. I want him to go and testify to my brother, lest he come to this awful place."

Don't you ever be ashamed of an old preacher. Don't you ever be ashamed of a fundamentalist who preaches hell, fire and brimstone. When your rich friends come to visit you don't go to the biggest church in town, bring them out here and get them saved. They will thank you through out eternity for it. "Send Lazarus that he may testify to my brethren, lest they come to this awful place of torment." Oh, he had concern for his brothers then after he was in hell, after it was too late.

Abraham said, "Son, they've got Moses and the prophets. That's the Bible. They've got Moses and the Prophets." He said, "Lord, they won't believe them, but if you send a man from the dead, they will believe him."

Abraham said, "If they won't believe the Bible, they wouldn't believe one who came from the dead." If you can't believe the Word of God, you wouldn't believe any sign or any miracle. The only thing that will ever get you saved is to believe in God's Word.

The Bible proves there is no need for any one to go to hell. The

237

most foolish thing, in the world, is for anyone to die without Jesus Christ. It is so simple and so wonderful to be saved. You may disagree with me, but that is all right. Of course, if you want to go through life being wrong, that's up to you.

I read a story a little while back about Napoleon who had a little old bugler boy one time and the battle was going bad. He looked up and saw his men being beaten. "Sound the retreat, call the men back." The boy stood there and said, "Sir, I can't do it, you never taught me how to sound the bugle for retreat. But I can sound a charge that will make a dead man get up and walk." Napoleon said, "Blow it son." The little boy stood there and began to blow and the sound went out across the hills and valleys. The soldiers got up and started forward toward the enemy, the enemies turned and fled. Napoleon's army won.

Go out and blow your bugle. Don't sound retreat. Sound a charge. Sound it so loud that folks will get up and walk. So dead men will walk, dead men in sin. That is what we need to do.

There is a hell, and the Bible proves it.

Be One In Jesus Christ

1 Corinthians 14:32-33, "And the spirits of the prophets are subject to the prophets, for God is not the author of confusion, but of peace as in all churches of the saints."

Among people who have inspirational experiences of prophecy, tongues, and interpretation of tongues, it is very easy for one to claim that the Holy Spirit is moving upon him and that he should not quench the spirit. This attitude of being determined to obey the spirit leads to abuse of such gifts many times, causing much confusion in the church.

Let no man claim to be moved by the Holy Spirit who acts disorderly and causes confusion, for God is not the author of such.

James 3:13-17, "Who is a wise man and endued with knowledge among you? Let him show out of a good conversation his works with meekness of wisdom. But if you have bitter envying and strife in your hearts, glory not, and lie not against the truth. This wisdom descends not from above, but is earthly, sensual, and devilish. For where envying and strife is, there is confusion and every evil works. But the wisdom that is from above is first pure, then peaceable, gentle, and easy to be entreated, full of mercy and good fruits, without partiality, and without hypocrisy."

A wise man is one who can bridle his own tongue, and is qualified to teach others. Control your conduct, actions, and your words. True wisdom from God is always accomplished with meekness and gentleness. Proud and overbearing men may pass as scholars and have learning, but not true wisdom from above. But if you are bitter, have envy; you do not have true wisdom. Even if you defend religion, you are false in your profession and lie against the truth. If you glory in professing wisdom, if you have only earthly things in view, if you have or cause confusion, then you are inspired by the wrong spirit, not God's spirit.

But the one with divine wisdom is pure, holy clean, peaceable, gentle, modest, and kind. They are not stubborn or obstinate, but full of mercy. They are always forgiving and performing acts of kindness, producing good fruits, without partiality and are open, honest, genuine and true.

Lately, too much attention has been put on Satan and not enough on Jesus Christ. Let us get our attention back on Jesus and Satan will not stick around.

Salvation does not come by Satan, but by Jesus Christ.

Jesus said in Luke 10:20, "Rejoice not, that the spirits are subject to you, but rather rejoice, because your names are written in Heaven." It is a natural tendency for man to glory in the exercise of power. But some causes price and leads to the downfall of a gifted man. Rejoice in the Holy Spirit, which is the true source of joy and will never result in spiritual pride that causes one's downfall.

Psalms 97:12, "Rejoice in the Lord, you righteous, and give thanks at the remembrance of His holiness." David says, "Hate evil, and don't be talking about it all the time. Rejoice in the Lord, give thanks to him and remember His holiness." Put God, put Jesus, put the Holy Spirit, back in the "spotlight," not Satan.

Psalms 86:11, "Teach me Your way, O Lord, I will walk in your truth. Unite my heart to fear your Name. In Matthew 10:28, "Fear not them which kill the body, but are not able to kill the soul, but rather fear Him which is able to destroy both soul and body in hell." Don't fear man and the evil of this world, they cannot destroy you. God is in command, He has the power to lift up and cast down.

Take a minute to read Philippians 2:1-8.

If you are to be like Christ, if you have love, if you wish to have Christ like fellowship with others, fulfill the joy of Christ, that you be like-minded, having the same love, being of one accord, or one mind. Be united in one mind, the mind of Christ. Love in the same degree and be in agreement in all things for the Master. Never oppose each other by acting for personal gain or having a self-glory.

Have a humbling view of yourselves, knowing your own secret faults and true self.

GRANDPA'S LESSONS ABOUT JESUS

Do not be selfish glorying in your own gifts and graces. Be just as interested in the blessings of others and rejoice to see them blessed.

Let the mind of self-emptying be in you, which was in Christ.

Be consecrated to humble yourself.

Jesus laid aside His divine form. Can we?

Jesus took the form of a servant. Can we? Have you?

Jesus was made in the likeness of men. Don't forget that you are still man.

Jesus humbled Himself. Can you? Do you?

Jesus became obedient to death, always obedient to the Heavenly Father. Are we? Are you?

Christ was also in the form of God. Do we conduct our personal services as Christ did? Do we conduct our church service, as Christ would, if He were in charge?

Is Christ in charge of your services? Or are you in charge?

Christ became a servant and became like man. Can turn that around, saying we are man and become like Christ?

Jesus was obedient to God His Father in all things, at all times and in all places.

Every tongue shall confess His Lordship to the glory of God. Are we letting Christ work through us? Or are we trying to do the work of Christ without Christ?

Is it, look at me, look at my power? Or is it, look what Christ is doing through me? Rejoice not, that the spirits are subject to you, but rather rejoice because your names are written down in Heaven.

Do not challenge Satan. Do not tempt Satan. Do not invite Satan to show you his power. In Egypt, Satan said to Moses, "Can you top this?" God's power is not for show, or to be used to show off.

Do not invite Satan to show you his power, but be prepared with the power of God, through the authority of Jesus, when he does attack you. Quit inviting the devil to attack you. If we go looking for Satan, he will find you and make himself known and challenge you.

Let us get our attention back on Jesus Christ, but stay alert to the actions of Satan.

You can be in one accord with everybody in your church; but if you are not in one accord with Jesus you will fail.

When you are not in unity. When you are not in one accord with Jesus, the devil will pick you off one at a time.

God is still in control. Let Him be in control.

A Reed, A Rock
Luke 22:31-33

Satan, the tempter and accuser of the brethren.

Satan has a desire to have you, that he may sift you as wheat. Satan, Jesus says, has demanded to obtain you by asking for you. This is what he did in Job's case, and God evidently granted him his request, and Satan wants control of your life, too. But Jesus adds, "I have prayed for you, that your faith will fail you not."

Satan, when your faith fails, wants to sift you as wheat, throws you into the air, back into the ways of the world. But Jesus said, "I have prayed for you, that your faith fail you not." Jesus also said, "I have prayed that when you are converted, you will strengthen your brethren." Strengthen the believer. O how dangerous it is, right after you believe and receive Jesus as your Lord and Savior. Satan tries real hard.

This does not mean that Peter had not been converted, for he had been and he had served God for over three years. It simply refers to the fact that he was headed for a fall; and that he would

244

come back to God and be reconverted, and becoming stronger than he was before.

Had Peter received the new birth?

John writes in 1 John, "If any man (Christian) sins he has an advocate with the Father." What is this advocate for, if not to restore backsliders to God?

Peter was once converted, confessing Jesus as the Son of God, which brings the new birth. Peter even had power to preach and heal and had the spirit in him. Jesus here today, predicts his backsliding, and re-conversion. Now this is proving that a converted person can and must be re-converted if he sins as Peter did in denying Jesus.

Paul taught that men who have erred from the truth, and who have even over thrown the faith of others, might come to repentance again. (2 Tim 2:17-26)

Peter said, "Lord, I am ready to go with you, both into prison, and to death." This kind of pride and boasting was the cause of Peter's downfall. Such is likely to happen to anyone who does not take heed.

Paul writes in 1 Corinthians 10:12-13, "Wherefore let him that thinks he stands take heed lest he fall. There has no temptation taken you, but such as is common to man; but God is faithful, who will not suffer you to be tempted above that you are able, but will with the temptation also make a way to escape, that you maybe ale to bear it."

This is a warning about backsliding and following the examples of Israel.

It also gives us the assurance of the eternal keeping of God in all temptations and His help in everyone of them, providing we obey the warnings. No man can be kept from a fall if he persistently refuses to meet conditions. Putting worldly things ahead of spiritual thing will surely lead to a fall. Our standing depends upon our faith and union with God and our steadfastness in prayer. The greatest saint can stand only as long as he depends upon God and continues in obedience to the gospel.

This is where we find Peter, here in Luke. Peter says, "I am ready. I am ready to go to prison to you. I am ready to die for you." But what does Jesus say? He said, "Listen to Me, Peter. I want to tell you something, Peter. The cock shall not crow this day, before that you shall three times deny that you know me."

Peter's pride and boasting was the cause of Peter's downfall. "No Lord, You are wrong, I am ready to follow you all the way." This was easy for Peter to say. Why?
Because:
1. He had Jesus as security there where he could see and touch Him.
2. He had preached, taught, and healed. His faith was sufficient. He had Jesus to tell back him up.
3. He thought, "I cannot backslide now." His pride was in himself, his boasting was in himself, and his faith was in self. No Lord I will not deny you, I am ready to follow you where ever.

246

GRANDPA'S LESSONS ABOUT JESUS

Luke 22:54-62, Peter:
- Boasted
- Lied, not Christ
- Slept instead of praying
- Relied on the arm of flesh
- Forsook Christ and fled
- Followed afar off
- Sat with the Lord's enemies
- Gave up hope, Discouraged
- He was afraid of men
- Lied
- Cursed

Jesus predicted all this (his backsliding), but also his re-conversion:

- Peter had been converted once.
- He was born again.
- Cleansed from sin and had kept God's Word.
- Name written in Heaven.
- Had eternal life.
- Had spiritual relations.
- Was in Christ.
- Was saved from the world.
- Had been baptized in water and had baptized others.
- Had the Holy Spirit.
- Had power over all kinds of sickness and demons.
- Had many other spiritual experiences that modern Christians do not have. So he needed re-conversion after backsliding like others had done.

The cock crowed, and the Lord turned and looked at Peter, and

GRANDPA'S LESSONS ABOUT JESUS

Peter remembered the Words of Jesus. Peter went out and wept bitterly.

If you are not serving God, you are serving Satan.

Jesus was crucified. Jesus was buried. Jesus lives again forever. Forty days Jesus walked and showed Himself on earth.

Now Jesus shows Himself to Peter again. John 21:15-17, "'Simon, son of Jonas, do you love Me more than these?' Peter said unto Jesus, 'Yes Lord, You know that I love You.' Jesus said, 'Feed my lambs.' Jesus said the second time, 'Simon, son of Jonas, Do you love Me?' Peter replied, 'Yes Lord, You know that I love you.' Jesus said, 'Peter, feed My sheep.'" (Sheep means lost men, saved men, and men in general.)

Jesus said the unto Peter the third time, "'Simon, son of Jonas, Do you love Me?' Peter answered Jesus, 'Lord you know all things, You know that I love You.' Jesus said unto Peter, 'Feed My sheep.'" It said that Peter was grieved when Jesus asked him the third time. Could Peter think that Christ knew something about him that he, himself, did not know, which might lead to another fall and was he about to tell him of it?

"Lord You know all things." This might have been the confession and the humility Christ was looking for. A few days before he knew more about himself that Christ did and was frank enough to say so. But his fall and repentance had greatly humbled him. Now he was not so sure of himself, but he was sure he loved Jesus.

Simon once the reed (one who sways from to side to side,

248

depending from which way the wind comes) now with Jesus as Peter the rock. (One who cannot be moved.)

Peter just gets himself out of the mess. He realizes that Jesus knows that he really loves Him. Jesus knows Peter's heart.

In John 21:20-25, Peter says, "Now Lord I have another question to ask You. Lord, what are you going to do about John? What is John going to do? You told me what to do, but now what about John?"

Jesus rebuked Peter's curiosity by stating that if He willed for John to live to the Second Advent, that was none of Peter's concern.

You follow Me and let John do likewise. Jesus or God never forces anyone to do anything. God gave man the freedom of choice and He will not take that freedom from him.

John 21:25, and there was so many things which Jesus did, the which, if they should be written everyone, I suppose that even the world itself could not contain the books that should be written. Amen.

Men in a lifetime could not even have time or take the time to study them or digest them.

Now, what about my neighbor, Lord? Let me change that question Lord. I mean what about me, Lord? Are we going to be a Simon or a Peter?

The Ideal Mother
Proverbs 31:10-31

Much talk of the old fashioned mother, and the question is asked, "Where is the old fashioned mother?" If the truth of the matter was really known, it's not so much the old fashioned mother that we are concerned about as it is the Ideal Mother.

There's a song that goes, "I want a girl, just like the girl that married dear old dad." In many cases we have had wonderful mothers, and we couldn't ask for better, but how about the countless thousands who cannot boast of such a mother?

The songs, which give all due respect to mothers, do not always fit all of them. How about the mother who sticks her baby in the garbage can, because she feels tied down? What about the mother-to-be, who gets an abortion, or how about the mother who neglects her family for a fling at the afternoon cocktail party with the "girls?" Or what about the mother who poisons the minds of her children with the dirt and gossip which she gathers by word of mouth and over the telephone? Many so-called old-fashioned mothers fall into these classes.

250

Really what we need today is not an old fashioned mother, but an Ideal Mother. Of course, we all have a standard for what we think the ideal mother should measure up to, but who can we say has the best standard? For the standard we must go to the time tested Book, the Bible, the Word of God. Here in the book of patterns we find the measuring stick of God applies. We find in Proverbs and we learn what God's standard is for the ideal mother:

1. Her values; chapter 31:10-11
   a. She must be worthy, one who possesses, and practices faith, hope, and charity. Also one who has fortitude, temperance, and justice.
   b. Hard to find. No street corner pick-up.
   c. Money can't buy her. Not a prostitute.
   d. One in whom her husband can trust.
2. Her vocation; verse 12-27
   a. Doing good. This was said of our Lord, who could set forth a better example.
   b. Works with her hands to provide for her family; sewing, cooking, etc.

"Happy Task"

Today I did my ironing.
The stacks were piled real high.
Some how it seemed no chore at all,
For God was standing by.

I talked with Him, and He with me.
My iron just fairly flew.
Before I knew it, I looked up
The stacks were almost through.

251

And as I ironed my clothes with love,
God's love did me enfold.
I knew that God was ironing too,
The wrinkles from my soul.

No greater work has mankind, than the work of a mother.

      c.   Teaches in wisdom and kindness, also surety of
           Heaven.
      d.   The best that a mother can give is her life. A woman
           sitting by herself on a train leaned over and to a
           woman who was traveling with two small children,
           "I'd give ten years of my life to have a couple of fine
           active youngsters like that." Then the mother
           responded, "That is just about what they cost."

The mother's victory: verse 28-31:
      a.   Her children are upright individuals.
      b.   She wins the favor of her children.
      c.   She is praised by her husband.
      d.   She reverences the Lord and is blessed by Him.
      e.   She is praised by those of her community.

Any woman who fears the Lord is to be praised. This is the
quality that is required of all mothers before she can be called of
God, "The Ideal Mother."

Some women want children; but do not want to be a mother to
them.

Romans 13:7: "Give honor and respect to all those to whom it
is due. Never finish paying your debt of love to God for your

mother." (Paraphrased)

Why do we need to be told to do this? Because, we are forgetful. Human beings need to be reminded. Some of us don't even remember her birthday or wedding anniversary. Every year on my birthday, I always sent my mother a thank you card for being a great mother to me for that amount of years.

Not only do we forget; we need to be told what is good, what is right and what true. We need to be reminded of the valid actions of our lives. And one of those valid things is honoring and paying respect to our mothers.

Now you ask why?

1. To her we owe our lives.
   a. Who does a baby recognize in its life first? Mom.
   b. She has more physical contact with us than any other.
   c. She laid her life on the line to give birth to us.
   d. Her health and well-being leaves its influence upon us. Look at the health, mental, moral, and physical of mothers, and see in many cases the effect upon her children, even in later life. Her spiritual influence has its effect in and upon their lives. What she does with her body, mind, and spirit affects the lives of all, with whom she comes in contact with. Children especially are great to mimic those they see and hear.

2. To her we owe the earliest part of our education.
   a. We learned to eat, to talk, to walk the first six years of our lives were dominated by her influence, and it was there we gained our learning experiences.

253

b. From her we learned to love and be loved. We learned the strength of a mother's love, and the risks it takes to love.

c. We learned obedience and respect for her and others.

d. We learned to pray, and the value of prayer.

e. We learned a language, first the ABC's etc.

f. We learned kindness and respect for others and their property and themselves as persons.

3. We are to honor her because:

a. This is where we first experienced home. It was more than a place to stay, to put up for the night. It was more than a place to sleep, or place to board and room for free.

b. Home is a center where a family lives together as a unit.

4. We honor her because she loved us before we loved her.

a. Her love, if it is real love, sustains us, and restrains us. It encourages us, and strengthens us in times of need and in time of plenty. Her love is like God's love. Even when we are often unlovely, she still loves us.

How can we honor her? First, by our affection. Second, by being today and every day, the men and women, boys and girls, with God's help, that our mothers want us to be. Amen?

Let every day be Mothers Day!
Make roses grow along her way,
And beauty everywhere.
Come grown children and rejoice,
That you can hear, your mother's voice.

GRANDPA'S LESSONS ABOUT JESUS

Let every day be Mothers Day!
With love and roses strew her way,
And smiles of joy and pride!
Come, grown-up children, to the knee
Where long ago you used to be
And never turn aside.
Oh, never let her eyes be wet
With tears because her babes forget.
       (Author unknown}

With Or Without Light

Light is used to shine on something so you can see it. Light is for safety, for beauty, and used for health. Light is for growing, to see direction, and for energy. Light is for revelation, such as x-ray, and for the expelling of darkness. Where is the darkness of the night when the sun comes up in the morning? The darkness goes nowhere. The light is stronger, like a road goes nowhere until we use it.

Light is used in almost every area of our daily life. There lights in the house, on the car, in the barn, and in the chicken house. We have a pole light for lighting our yard and security.

There are flasher lights at railroad crossings, signal lights at street intersections, directional lights at the air base to guide the aircraft to and from the base safely. I believe it would be almost impossible for us to live in such a complex life, without the aid of lights.

I wonder what you would say if when you go to purchase a new car and the salesman quoted a price on the car, and he said,

"Now do you want a price with lights or without lights?" I am sure you would ask him to quote you a price with lights, because a car without lights cannot be driven safely at night.

Yet there are those countless thousands of men and women driving down the highway of this world without the Light of the World, Jesus Christ.

Every day you and I read in the paper, hear on the radio, and see on our televisions the wrecks and the tragedies that have happened because people are driving without the Light of the World.

In Matthew 5:14-16, Jesus says, "You are the light of the world. A city that is set on a hill cannot be hid. Neither do men light a candle and put it under a bushel, but on a candlestick. Then it gives light unto all that are in the house. Let your light so shine before men, that they may see your good works, and glorify your Father which is in Heaven."

Jesus points out three things concerning Christians as lights.
1. Our value, "You are the light." You are that which illuminates, lights up, and dispels darkness. The only way that a lamp is of any value in the darkness is when it is burning. You might have ten lamps in every room in your home, but their value is only noticed when they are burning. What we have is not reflected light, but radiated through our lives, that which has been communicated to us from the Essential Light, Jesus Christ.

2. It is only as we are ignited and burn that others are able to see the Light of Jesus Christ, which shines through us.

We are transmitters of the Light of Jesus. We are not reflectors. Our light must shine from within us.

3. Even the furnace will not work without a flash of light from inside. An automobile engine will not work without a flash of light from the inside of the engine. A welder will not work without a flash of light.

In John 8:12 Jesus says, "I am the light of the world. He that follows Me shall not walk in darkness, but shall have the light of life."

In John 1:4 we read, "In Jesus was life, and the life was the light of men. And the light shined in darkness, and the darkness comprehended it not."

It says, Jesus is the Light; but the darkness of the world comprehended it not. Because of the powers of Satan the world could not discover or detect the light, Jesus Christ.

But in the beginning was the Word and the Word was with God and the Word was God. The same was in the beginning with God. But the darkness of Satan, or of the world, did not overcome the Word, but the Word spoiled the darkness on the cross. Of course the Word being, Jesus Christ Himself.

Jesus says in John 9:5, "As long as I am in the world, I am the Light of the world."

In John 12:35 Jesus says, "Yet a little while is the Light with you, walk while you have the Light, lest darkness comes upon you. For he that walks in darkness, knows not where he goes. While you have Light, believe in the Light, that you may be children of Light."

Let your light shine everywhere in the world, every area of life, and into all men everywhere. Wherever there is darkness. Even to men who are drifting about in the fog of life. Driving in fog calls for a different degree of light. You cannot use bright light in a fog, for if you do the moisture droplets will repel the light. Dim lights must be used of yellow or amber, so that the fog will absorb it allowing those who travel in it to find their way through it.

The only song that seems to please many of us is, "When we all get to Heaven." How about, "Work for the night is coming?"

Some times we can shine our lights too bright and it blinds those in darkness. "Let your light so shine before men that they may see your good works, and glorify your Father which is in Heaven."

Do not shine the light upon yourself, but be the light.

We as a church of Jesus Christ, need to be seen, and will be if we do what is required of us. We as a church need to flash our light everywhere.

We are as individual candles in our own homes. Radiating our light in private places. You may say, I can't be a city, but you can be an influence in which place you may be.

Let your light so shine before men that they may see your good works. "That they may see Jesus Christ in you, and glorify your

GRANDPA'S LESSONS ABOUT JESUS

Father which is in Heaven."

Is there anyone who would do without light in your own home? Well then, what about the Light of the world, which lights the soul into eternal life. (John 8:12)

Jesus said, "I am the Light of the world, he that follows Me shall not walk in darkness, but shall have the Light of Life."

If you are here and have received the Light of Life, will you do what Jesus commands you to do? Will you let your light shine? Will you let it shine wherever you may be?

If you are here without the Light of the world, will you come and allow Jesus to ignite you so that you too might burn and illumine the pathway of Life, so that you may no longer stumble in the dark?

Jesus said, "I am the Light of the world."
Jesus said, "I go to be with the Father."
Jesus said, "Now you are the light of the world."

The Light shows us the Way.
The Light keeps us from stumbling and falling.
The Light keeps others from stumbling over us.
The Light lets others see us.
Sin always seeks the darkness.
Sin is always hiding in shame, in a guilty feeling.

Have you let Jesus light your life?
If not, will you?

Life Is Like A Ship Upon The Sea
Luke 8:22-25 and Mark 4:37-41

One of the most beautiful and yet treacherous bodies of water in the world is the Sea of Galilee. It is situated some 500 feet below sea level and is only 80 or 90 miles from the lowest spot on the surface of the earth, which is the Dead Sea. Its waters can be so peaceful and calm that you could think that it would never encounter any storms. Yet within a matter of five or ten minutes, that same water can become turned into a hellish fury, so that no ship of the type that sail it, can survive unless it gets to the shore quickly. It's that kind of sea.

One evening when Jesus thought it was time to go across to the Land of Gadara, where He was to meet Legion and to cast all the demons out of him and then bring revival to the Dadarenes. He called these disciples of His to Him, and He said, "Let us go over to the other side." Now the very language He used is expressive of His faith and of His determination not to be defeated in the evening time, because one in that day did not ordinarily take a journey across the Sea of Galilee in the evening time. They usually took it during the daylight so if they

261

encountered a storm they could quickly find the shore.

Some of these disciples had been commercial fisherman. They knew the sea. They knew it like they knew the back of their hand. They not only loved it, but they respected and feared it. Jesus knew their thoughts, what was racing through their minds. "Why must we go at this time of day? Does He not know that this is the most dangerous time of the day to take such a trip?" And as if He knew their thoughts (and truly He did), He said, "Let us go over to the other side."

These are great words because they are symbolic of all the words of Jesus, to people, when it is a divine human, when it is God and man joining together in a cooperative venture, when He said, "Let us."

Jesus joined with them. He took His stand by their side. He would enter the boat as their divine companion. "Let us," He said. Then, knowing the terror they would experience in a few hours, He said, "Let us go over." And when He said, "Let us go over," that meant they could not go under.

Over not under. So Jesus and the disciples sailed away. Sure enough, they hit a storm. Storms come to us all, whether we are right or wrong, whether we are just or unjust. Not any different than the rain falling on the good and the bad alike. What difference then does it make for a man to serve God if he encounters the same kind of storms that other people do? Just this, Jesus Christ is in your boat, and that makes all the difference in the world.

The old storm struck in its fury. The winds began to howl, the

GRANDPA'S LESSONS ABOUT JESUS

Thunder crashed, the lightning flashed. Pretty soon the waves were churning, and the boat was rocking and the water was splashing over on the inside. It got ankle deep and knee deep, and then it came up until the boat was almost filled. The sails were almost ripped from the mast. The timbers of the deck began to pop, and the sides of the boat began to creak and all of a sudden these disciples were faced with sudden death.

When Jesus came aboard, He took His pillow, and went back into the back of the ship, laid His head upon the pillow, with His faith and slept like a baby. He knew He wasn't going under, but He was going over.

In the midst of the storm, when the winds were howling and the water was rolling and the thunder was crashing, the disciples went to pieces. They forgot that He was on board. Their imagination ran wild. Their fear struck like a dagger. They surveyed the situation, and they knew they were in mortal danger. Everything they knew came to their minds. We will never make it to the shore. We are out here in the middle of this sea, in the midst of a storm, and we will never get out alive.

The very treachery of the sea played upon their imagination. They became afraid, and their fear was traceable partly to their knowledge of the sea and the power of the elements, and partly to the fact that the elements now were out of control.

I think helplessness is the first reaction people have when trouble strikes. I know it is the first one I have at different times when I've had my back to the wall, my first reaction usually is to ask, "Where am I according to the natural way of doing things? What can I do? Who can help me? Who has an answer to bring

263

me out of this physically?"

The disciples ran up against the blank wall of helplessness because there wasn't anything that anybody could do, and they cried out with fear. It was not response to God. It was a reaction, and we can say we don't blame them because we probably would react in an identical way if we were in a similar situation. But later, when Jesus was awakened and came on the scene, He asked them two questions: "Why are you so fearful?" and "Where is your faith?"

He said their reaction to the storm could not be traced to the elements. Their reaction was bound up with their fear and faith.

We do not like to lay the blame where it should be. We do not like to find the truth in the matter. We human beings don't always want the truth? How many times when we pray for the sick, we find that people would rather talk to us than have us pray for them. They would rather have our sympathy than our compassion. Sympathy is a human thing, while compassion is divine. Sympathy says, "Oh, I'm sorry." "Oh did that happen to you?" "Oh, what a terrible thing."

Some would rather have me talk like that. Now compassion is divine. Compassion springs from a Godly love, Love that is unmotivated. God said, "Love your enemies." Love them in spite of them, not because they are your enemies, but in spite of that fact. Love a Godly love, reaches down to the people who are in need. Compassion stirs you, and wakes you want to do something about it.

When I pray for the sick, the moment I have sympathy, I am

dead. I can't help anybody. Sympathy usually makes people sicker than what they are, because they just wilt.

Compassion is doing something. When I pray for the sick and feel compassion, my hand wants to touch people. I want to pray against the sickness; I want God to cast it out. I want to do something about it, and this is what we must face. Do we want sympathy, or do we want compassion? No sickness is strong enough to resist the healing of God; but many people through themselves remain completely outside of their healing.

The disciples finally awakened Christ and accused Him of not caring. I think that is part of our reaction. I think I've done the same thing in my life. For the first reaction at trouble or sickness or some disaster in our personal lives is, "God doesn't care for me, He doesn't know I live." That is a human reaction, and that's why we need God, because our human reaction is wrong.

When Jesus was aroused from His sleep, He walked up on deck and saw the situation. He asked just two Questions. "Why? Why are you scared to death?" "We are going to be killed," they replied. Then Jesus said, "Where is your faith?"

Now He acted, He had the thing under control. He walked up as if it was the most natural thing in the world for a human to look at his problems and solve them. Problems are to be solved. We are not to be victims of our problems. We are not to be a bound under their heels. God didn't make us to be the tail, but to be the head. God gave us dominion, and Christ came to heal. Christ came to save. Christ came to cast out demons, not to have demons ruling our lives. Christ came to supply our needs, not to have us ground in the dust of poverty all our lives. God came to do something for us, not to have us beneath His feet.

Well, why are we scared? And I ask myself, just like I ask you, "Why are we scared, and where is our faith?"

Jesus said the whole thing deals with our faith and our fear. Now these men believed all the time. And what did they believe? That God didn't care? "Master do you care not that we perish?" They were going to perish, and they believed that they were all alone. But what they believed wasn't true. They were not alone, because Christ was on board. They were not going to perish because God said, "You cannot go under for going over." That shows you how our believing can play tricks on us.

This is where our fear comes from. Fear comes from our wrong believing. Do you realize that faith and fear come from the same source? They come from our believing. We believe wrong and we have fear. We believe right and we have faith.

You put your hand on the gearshift in your car, and that hand can shift forward or into reverse. You move that shift one-way with that hand and the car goes forward. You take your hand and move that same gearshift another direction and the car will move in reverse. It makes no difference how light or hard you step on the accelerator, that car is going the way you shift the gear.

Folks, we are dealing with reality. We're dealing with sin and disease and demons that would destroy us. We are dealing with fear. We must find out what our problem is and why we are not getting it solved; and nine out of ten times, our belief is flawed. We believe that God doesn't care, and that's a lie. The

266

Resurrection sings the story that God does care. The death of Jesus Christ tells us that God cares. God rolled the stone from the mouth of a cave, and brought Him out victorious. This shows that God cares for us. Heaven bent low for us on Pentecostal morning and poured out the gift of the Holy Ghost. That shows that God cares.

When we feel that God doesn't care, our feelings are lying to us. God cares. People say that we are going to perish. Well, there is only one way that we can perish and that is to be outside of Jesus Christ.

We've got to follow what our heart tells us. We've got to obey the Lord. There comes a time when a man has to obey. He has to put his faith into action. And the disciples said right back, "Why, don't You care? Don't You care?" And Jesus answered right back, "Why are you scared? Just give Me the reason?"

Then Jesus said, "Where is your faith? If you had faith you wouldn't have this fear. Where is your faith?" Some people will come up to me, and put up their hands and say, "All right, let's see what you can do."

I can't do a thing, not do a thing in the world. But, oh, when we come and destroy fear and let our faith out, something invisible breaks loose in the atmosphere.

God's power spins this universe. God reached out His hand and made a scoop, and the oceans were made. God flung out His hand and the planets came into orbit. God moved his fingers and the mountains were sculptured. He can surely reach down and heal our bodies now. He can save our souls. He can deliver us.

Jesus walked up through the water, swirling around His body, to the bow of the ship. He stood there surveying the elements. He heard the crack of the thunder and saw the flash of the lightning. The wind blew His garments about Him, and it began to flap against His body. He could scarcely hold His stand, but He put His arm and His hand up, and he spoke three words: "Peace, be still." And He hushed the sea to sleep. It was all over.

When they got to shore they looked at Him and they said, "What manner of man is this?"

He was a man as a baby in His mother's arms, but He was God, when He took the broken bodies and broken souls and minds and put them together. He was God, when the salty tears ran down His cheeks because of the death of His friend Lazarus. He was God, and He cried out, "Lazarus, come forth."

He was man when He cried on the cross, "I thirst." He was God when He walked out and said, "Because I live, you shall live also."

The disciples said, "What manner of man? He commands the seas and winds and they obey." They said, "Look at Him. He commands the sea, He commands the wind, and they obey."

A man gets so far in his sin that his sin possesses him, and this drives him, and no matter how much he wants to be free and change, he can't change until he meets Jesus. Jesus commands, and sin goes.

GRANDPA'S LESSONS ABOUT JESUS

A man gets so sick, a woman gets so sick, that they can't lift their head with cancer or something else. Their bodies swell and they hurt badly, or they have arthritis, or they're going blind, or they're gripped with sickness and nothing will drive the sickness out.

Jesus commands, and the disease goes out of the body. It leaves the joints, and it leaves the blood and leaves the nervous system.

The demons control, and he rages and he foams at the persons mouth, and he throws the person down, and he wastes his strength and his body strength diminishes from day to day. But Jesus commands, and the demons are cast out. What manner of man is this? He is God. He is the only One who can deliver you. When Christ is in you, you are a winner. You will never fail. You are always a winner with Jesus. With Jesus all things are possible.

Just Looking

Christianity is not a spectator religion.

Jeremiah 29:13: "You shall seek Me, and find Me, when you shall search for Me with all your heart."

You couldn't stay in business very long if people were just looking. In the stores are countless hundreds, "just looking." The clerks ask, "May I help you?" "May I wait on you?" And the people answer, "No thank-you, I'm just looking." Everyone is asked daily by the opportunities that confront them, "May I help you? Something for you?"

Jesus says, "May I help you?' Then most of us answer Him and say, "No, not right now, I'm just looking." All have to plead guilty, "Not now, I'm just looking." We have opportunities to help, to serve, to give and to be kind and share or to be responsible, but we say, "Really, Lord, I'm not ready yet. I want to look around a little more. I'm just looking Lord."

Some people go all the way through life, just looking. Now

something good, I suppose, can be said about just looking.

1.) It's less expensive than buying. You don't put forth any effort. It doesn't cost anything. You pay nothing. You give nothing.
2.) If you don't buy, you don't have to use it. You can't lose it. We may sit still. We have no responsibilities.
3.) Remember, God gave us eyes and we ought to use them for enjoyment of things, not responsibility to God, or to others or to self.

But if we analyze these excuses, are they any good?

"Just looking" started rather unconsciously when toddlers start talking. Watch a youngster get into things, why does he do it? Ask him and he will tell you, "Just looking." Look in an old trunk in the attic or in an old box at a sale. Is there something hidden in there? Why are we looking? Because we are seeking something, we know not what.

God set a hunger in man's heart. You and I know a hunger, which bread cannot satisfy, a thirst that water cannot quench.

Every year puzzled people spend over a hundred million dollars in our United States use astrology, palm readers, and fortune tellers tell them the wrong answers to their hearts questions. They are seeking. Nearly 20,000 of these puzzled people gave up in despair and chose suicide to escape the questions of life. Untold thousands found themselves in the mental institutions of our land. Millions of others spent billions in belief that the corner tavern was the nearest escape route.

271

But to no avail, awoke the next morning with bloodshot eyes, muddy minds, empty wallets and throbbing heads. Today it is marijuana, speed, LSD, and other drugs. Why are people buying these things? Because of only one reason, they say that they are "Just looking" for answer.

I know you have all heard this scripture, because I sent it to most of you at one time. Matt 7:7-23:

Ask: To beg, to desire, to require of demand. We must ask with confidence and humility.

Seek: With the whole heart, implies loss. Seek with care, and diligence.

Knock: Implies a need, an urgent need. Knock with earnestness and perseverance. Pound on God's door and say, "Lord this devil is after me. Open the door Lord. If there are limitations in an answer, there is limitation of faith. Not God's will or Power.

Matthew 7:15 says, "Beware of false prophets, which come to you in sheep clothing, but inwardly they are as ravishing wolves." Jesus said, "Keep away from false prophets, and keep away from false teachers."

There are seven ways in which false prophets or teachers are known:

1. By outward general conduct.
2. By inward state.
3. By the kind of fruit it is work is producing. What is the result of your teaching, confusion or peace?
4. By the kind of fruit in doctrine taught. What are you teaching?

272

5. By professing to do, but not doing the will of God. And do not say that you cannot know the will of God. For He left a Will. The Holy Bible.
6. By Satan's backing, who is backing the words you teach?
7. By the destiny they are seeking or headed for.

A man cannot be a saint and a sinner at the same time.

Every tree that does not bring forth, good fruit, will be cut down and cast into the fire. No person, merely professing faith in Me and My atoning work will be saved, "but he that does the will of My Father."

We have become a generation of empty souls. We have lost true sight of what Jesus said, "Man shall not live by bread alone, but by every word that proceeds from the mouth of the Father." The secret lies in what many have discovered, "God has made us for Himself, our hearts are restless until they find rest in God."

Jesus has brought to us the answers to our problems of sin, sorrow, and death. For sin, He has given us forgiveness. For sorrow, the divine comfort of a God who suffers with His children. For death, abundant life, eternal, that begins here and now and continues forever.

Christ remains as constant as God's love.

Jesus offered no mere painkillers, no changed circumstances, no exemption from temptation, sorrow suffering or even death. Even as he endured all, so must we. Jesus promised power to live through these and to triumph over these as we walk in faith with God the Father.

273

GRANDPA'S LESSONS ABOUT JESUS

But man keeps looking elsewhere for the answers.

God's Word to us is: "And you shall seek Me, and find Me, when you shall search for Me with all your heart.

We have what many are looking for: "We have the answer in Jesus." Here we have the answer in the Word of God. "Whosoever shall drink of this water shall never thirst again." (meaning the Holy Spirit)

"Just Looking?"

Jesus says, "Don't just look, Ask, seek, and knock."

Are we just looking? "Or are we seeking?"
Are we false prophets, false teachers?
Are we doing it for our own personal Glory?

Are we doing it for the glory of God and His Church?

What does it mean to seek God, and find Him?
It means:
1. I must seek truth and do it.
2. I must seek righteousness and be righteous.
3. I must seek holiness and be holy.

Looking at truth is far different from doing truth. God calls us all to truth, righteousness and holiness.

Jesus comes to you today. He is saying, "May I help you please?" "May I serve you?" "Will you let me?" "Will you follow me?"

What is your answer? "Is it, Lord, I am just looking."

Or is it, "Yes Lord, I found what I am seeking, I found You. Let me walk with you."

The Compassion of Jesus

"But when He saw the multitude, He was moved with compassion." (Matthew 9:36)

The key to the earthly ministry of Jesus Christ was compassion. You have to follow Him in His journeys by day and by night to find the proof of this statement.

Whether He ministers to the sick of the palsy, or turns aside to the father whose child is dead. Whether He heals the woman with the issue of blood, or drives away the leprosy from the man dead by law. Whether He stops to open the eyes of the blind, or helps the beggar, or wins the member of the Sanhedrin. Jesus was always the same. Jesus is always the same. "One with compassion."

If you walk with Jesus in the morning on the shores of the Sea of Galilee, if you rest with Him at noon as He sits at the well that Jacob built. If you stop with Him in the evening as He bares His side and thrusts forth His hand to the doubting Thomas. Or if you behold Him as He is roused from His sleep in the boat to quiet the storm. If you study Him on the mountain at midnight or behold Him in the garden of Gethsemane when no one beholds His agony; but the eyes of the Father; you will learn that Jesus is always compassionate.

You cannot discover Him under any circumstances when this statement is not true of Him. Everywhere, all times.

The ninth chapter of Matthew is indeed remarkable. It can be appreciated only when we read the closing part of the eighth chapter, for it is here that the people, angry because of the destruction of the swine, brought Him to leave their country. And it is here, we see Him taking His departure. Men have, since that time, driven Jesus from their hearts and their homes for reasons quite as trifling. It is a sad thing to know that any one can drive Jesus away if he chooses to do so.

I think this chapter is remarkable, however, because there we not only read the story of the calling of the Matthew from his position of influence, but find more specific cases of healing than in most other chapters of the new testament.

There is the healing of the sick of the palsy, in the second verse, the part that stands out is he was healed when Jesus saw their faith: "The faith of his friends."

The picture of the Father, whose child was dead, and then raised from the dead.

The account, of the woman with the issue of blood, in the twentieth verse, and in the picture of discouragement when all earthly physicians had failed, changed into great joy, when the virtue of The Great Physician healed her.

The account of the dumb man, in the 32nd verse, who was possessed of a devil, Jesus healed as well.

There was a general statement in the 35th verse concerning him to the effect that He healed all manner of diseases.

The chapter is also remarkable because these cases presented to Jesus were of the worst sort. The man with the palsy could not come himself, however much He ever wanted to do so, and four men were required to bring him.

The child was dead and so beyond all human help. The two blind men were surly, beggars and outcasts. The dumb man was possessed of a devil in addition to his dumbness.

The group of people, who were subjects of His healing power, had every manner of disease, but while the people were different, and in the cases were desperate, Jesus was always the same.

Notice now. There were six specific illustrations of healing. Three of these came to Jesus for themselves.
1. The two blind men.
2. The woman with the issue of blood.

The others were brought to Him.
1. The sick man with the palsy.
2. The man who was dumb.

And the other case the father came and took Jesus to the child.

278

In all general cases Jesus went Himself to the suffering. When all these subjects have been presented, then comes the text, "But when Jesus saw the multitude, He was moved with compassion."

There is first the picture of the multitude. Great number of people, then the statement that they had fainted, literally it was saying, "They were tired."

Then they were described as sheep, "The only animal known which in its wandering cannot find its way home by itself." Then finally it was stated that they had no shepherd. The responsibility for their wandering rested upon others rather than upon themselves.

The picture, which Jesus saw as He walked through His own country is repeated today on every side of us, and He is still moved with compassion, because of those who are helpless, without Jesus.

It is true that the church machinery of the day is well near perfect. With the buildings and resources with which we have to do, have never been greater. Yet counting the membership of both the Catholic and Protestant churches, there are millions of people today in the United States who are not in the church and who do not care for the church. To these people there seems to be a growing indifference to everything that is spiritual.

In every city, it is true that there are thousands of unchurched people without God and without hope in the world. Of them the text would be true, "But when He saw the multitude He was moved with compassion."

GRANDPA'S LESSONS ABOUT JESUS

When Jesus saw these multitudes He saw them fainting or "growing tired' and this is the picture of lost people today. I am persuaded that they are tired of many things, which follow in the wake of sin.

In the Old and New Testament, God's people are represented by the figure of sheep, which is especially fitting, because sheep, when wandering, find it impossible to seek again for themselves, their home, and in their helplessness they fittingly represent the ones who wanders away from God. There are so many people today who are trying to find their way back without Christ. They are like wandering sheep. There are so many, who are seeking to climb up some other way into the favor of God. These are on every side of us, and the time has come for us to present unto them Jesus Christ the Savior of the world.

Jesus sent out workers to reach the lost.

I read somewhere that of the forty distinct cases of healing in the New Testament only six came to Jesus by themselves. Twenty were brought to Jesus. Jesus was taken to the other fourteen.

I imagine the proportion is the same today, and if it is true then our methods of work must be changed and instead of praying for them to seek Jesus by themselves, we must either take them to Jesus, or bring the Master into their company. There can be no successful winning of the multitudes until the personal element enter in it all.

One on one, one on one, do you hear me? Did I say one on one? Yes I said "One on one."

Where is God's Church located? Wherever two or three are gathered together in Jesus' Name. (Matt 18:20)

The one on one method is mainly what Jesus used. He said, "Your faith has made you whole."

We have friends who possess eyes and see not. We must have eyes for them. They have lips and speak not; we must speak to God with and for them. They have hands and reach them not out to God, we must reach out with them. In other words, we must not let them go away from Christ. Such a spirit as pleases God and such a spirit saves our friends.

When we come across a soul that had once been lost as we walk upon the streets of glory, upon the streets of gold, we will know that they are there because we were true; and because we cared, the streets of gold will be better, the gates of pearl will be brighter, the many mansions more beautiful, the music sweeter, and if such a thing was possible the vision of Christ more entrancing.

Certainly it would be thrilling to hear Him say to us, "In as much as you did it unto these little ones, you did it unto Me."

Who Cares?
Luke 10:1-9

John 9:11: "The Man called Jesus made clay and anointed my eyes and I received my sight."

In Nottingham, England stands the Chapel where William Booth, the founder of the Salvation Army, was converted. A memorial tablet commemorates the experience that made him forevermore the friend of the friendless. One who in the Name of Christ cared for those rejected by others and in need of help.

One day an old man in the uniform of the Salvation Army stood in front of this memorial. He knelt, bowed his head and prayed, "O God, do it again. Do it again."

Today when there is so much personal indifference to need, we hear voices everywhere crying out, "Who cares?" Who cares that men and women are growing old and are frightened and lonely? Who cares that in these days of affluence there are persons who are sick, and cannot afford the medical care they so desperately need? Who cares that one person out of five must be treated for mental illness during his lifetime? Who cares about the many children who are emotionally scarred by tragedies our society spawns?

We say that our Churches care as it provides homes for the aging, services to children and youth, and hospitals and medical centers to heal the hurting and the sick, but is it enough that our church cares? Are we as individuals blind to the needs of our neighbors, those near and those we never see?

When we recall the experience in which Jesus made clay, He anointed the eyes of the blind man and caused him to see, we want to pray that He will open our eyes so that we may see. Like the old man in the chapel we want to pray that He will move our hearts so that we may care.

"O, God, do it again, to me."

Take time to read Luke 10:1-9.

The men whose lives fill the pages of the New Testament, looked upon themselves as belonging to a fellowship, not a fellowship of what we call a good time, but "the fellowship of His sufferings;" which is the most worthy society to which one can belong. It involves more that a building made with hands. It means more that a church where people maintain a cultivated standard of social life. It means the whole-minded dedication to the purpose of Jesus. When our Lord made His final journey to Jerusalem, He was going to test whether by suffering He could bring God and man, and man and man together.

We believe that each member, where he lives and works is the church. We believe that if he is representative of Christ, this will have evangelistic implications to all around Him. We believe the world is being influenced, not by a few active leaders in the church, but by all of its members. We believe that we are all witnesses to the effectiveness or ineffectiveness of the Gospel in our lives.

Why then is the Church in the world? Why should I care?

In Luke 10:1-9, the Lord appointed, we do not choose, and we choose to obey or not obey. He appointed seventy also, so this makes 82 preachers and healers. He sent them two by two, to strengthen each other in weakness, for unity in prayer, and for protection in attack. He sent them in pairs for confirmation in preaching.

Both the laborers and the Harvesters are true emblems of the Christian and his work of winning souls. Look for the need of the people and take that need to God and see that it is met, so I send out harvesters. Jesus said to be kind so that men will see Me in you.

Say, "Peace be to this house." This is the usual salutation in entering a home. So Jesus is saying, "be courteous."

In verse nine Jesus says, "Heal the sick that are there in, and say unto them the kingdom of God is come nigh unto you."

They were commissioned to heal all the sick in every city they entered as proof that the kingdom of God had come to them and that God's representatives were in their midst. How we need such representation today. The kingdom of God is still not in word only, but in power and Jesus gives you this power through the Holy Spirit if you will only believe and accept it.

Why should I care?

So men may hear Christ's call. The Lord appointed men to go forth. Today God still appoints men and in every generation. If you are a believer, God has appointed you to go forth and work for Him. We need to hear to become aware. Men are lost without Christ, and there is the need. We need to hear and to become aware of man's need and the answer is God.

We are the advertising agents of the gospel. We are to make you aware of our produce and our product is Jesus Christ. Jesus Christ's produce is love. Some preachers try to get you to buy salvation, healing love, etc. Jesus says this is free. First we must come to know that there is a God and then we must come to know the God that is. Then we must care and share.

How good do you present Jesus in your talk and in your everyday living?

You are God's Church. Wherever you are that men may hear Christ's call. That man may accept Christ's grace. That man may do Christ's work. This is why we have the church. This is why the church is in the world. This is why the labors in the world and remember you are the church.

We call to Jesus and ask, "Lord, open our eyes, open our ears, open our mouth, open our hands, open my heart." My friend He has already done this on the Cross.

For the Lord your God is Holy. (Lev 19:2)

Only God is Holy.
Only God is complete, whole and hallowed.
Only God is totally worthy of our adoration.
There is danger that lesser gods of human origin will mar our relationship with the one true God.
Consecrate yourselves and be Holy. (Lev 20:7)

As God's children we must strive for holiness, without which we cannot see the Lord.
Be Holy yourselves in all your conduct: (1Peter 1:15)

Holiness in our lives is an inner experience, but it does not end there. Personal holiness should be visible when our neighbors and friends see us in the daily round they should be encouraged to look beyond and above and see the holiness of God.

How do you labor? Who do you labor for?

The Power Of The Spoken Word

I would like to talk to you today about the power of the spoken word, the power of God's Word, as well as the power of your own words. Your word has power. God's Word had power and still has power today.

In the beginning God created the heavens and the Earth. And the earth was without form and void, and darkness was upon the face of the deep. And the Spirit of God moved upon the face of the waters. And God said, "Let there be light." And there was light. And God said, "Let there be a firmament (clouds containing water) in the midst of the waters, and let it divide the waters from the waters." And God called the firmament heaven.

And God said, "Let the waters under the heaven be gathered together unto one place, and let the dry land appear," and it was so. And God called the dry land earth and the gathering of the waters He called seas, and saw that it was good.

And God said, "Let the earth bring forth grass, the herb yielding seed, and the fruit tree yielding fruit after his kind," and it was so. And God said, "Let there be lights in the firmament of the heavens, to divide the day from night, and let them be for signs, seasons, and for days, and years." And God made two great lights, the greater to rule the day and lesser to rule the night, He made the stars also. And God set these two lights in the heavens to give light upon the earth. And God saw it was good.

And God said, "Let the waters bring forth abundantly the moving creatures that has life, and fowl that may fly above the earth in the open firmament, of the heaven." And God created the great whales, and every living creature that moves in the water and every winged fowl and God saw it was good.

And God said, "Let the earth bring forth the living creature after his kind cattle, and every creeping thing that creeps upon the earth." And it was so.

And God said, "Let Us make man in our own image, after Our likeness. And let them have dominion over the fish of the sea, over the fowl of the air, over the cattle, and over every living thing creeping upon the earth." So God created man in His own Image, in the Image of God created He him. Male and female created He them. And God blessed them, and God said, "Be fruitful and multiply and replenish the earth and have dominion over the fish of the sea, the fowls of the air, and over every living thing that moves upon the face of the earth." And God saw everything He had made and said, "It is very good."

And the Lord formed man of the dust of the ground and breathed into his nostrils the breath of life and man became a living soul. Now I repeat what I told you many times before, "Man was made out of the dust of the ground, and until God breathed into him the breath of life, man was nothing but dirt."

Now my point is that God created everything, the heavens, the earth, the sun, the moon, the stars, and the whole universe according to His Spoken Word. His Word is true. If God would take back His Word this all would disappear.

We cannot understand how He did it with His Word, but His Word has power and this is what He gave us in the Bible, in which we learn that we were created in the image of God, and therefore our word also has power. We do not realize the power we have.

It has been told that God has created the sun and the moon, and we are somewhat like this. God representing the sun and us representing the moon and we should reflect the Word of God. Like the moon reflects the sun's light, but this is not what God says. God did not make man as reflectors, but God made man as transmitters. The sun (God) is the transmitter of His Word. God did not make man as reflectors, for reflectors reflect from the outside, but transmitters transmit from the inside. We must be transmitters not reflectors of his Word, but mindful that our own words have power.

In the Gospel of John, John writes, "In the beginning was the Word, and the Word was with God and the Word was God." The same was in the beginning with God. He made all things, and without Him there would be nothing. In Him was life, and life was the light of man (remember God breathed into man the breath of life).

And John continues in the 12th verse of Chapter 1, "But as many as received Him. To them gave He power to become the sons of God, even to them that believe on His name. Which were born not of blood, nor of the will of the flesh, nor of the will of man, but of God." The word of God benefits only the individual who has received Him, and the individual becomes the Son of God by adoption, not as God's begotten Son. For Jesus was the only begotten Son of God as we see in John 3:16, "For God so loved the world, that He gave His only begotten Son, that whosoever believes in Him should not perish, but have everlasting life. For God sent not His Son into the world, to condemn the world; but that the world through Him might me saved."

But back to the first chapter of John, "And the Word was made flesh, and dwelt among us, and we beheld His glory, the Glory as of the only begotten of the Father, full of grace and truth."

And John bears witness of this; Jesus was the living Word of God. The Word has power. God's Word has power. Therefore Jesus being God's Word, God's living Word, God's Son, Jesus has power. Therefore since we are made in the Image of God and we are adopted sons of God, we may make use of the power of God's Word.

Psalms 107 starting with the 15th verse reads, "Oh that men would praise the Lord for His goodness, and for His wonderful works to the children of men. Fools because of their transgression, and because of their iniquities, are afflicted. Their souls abhor all manners of meat, and they draw near to the gates of death. Then they cry unto the Lord in their trouble, and he saves them out o their distresses. He sent his Word and healed them, and delivered their destruction." Again we see the Power of the "Word of God." For it says "God sent His Word and delivered them and healed them and delivered them from their destruction."

In Matthew 8:16 we read, "When the evening was come they brought unto Jesus many that were possessed with devils; and He cast out the spirits, <u>with His Word</u>. And He healed all that were sick." Here we see Jesus through His word, through His Father's Word (which He said I can do nothing without My Father), through His Word, He healed the sick, cast out the demons, and freed the demon possessed.

Our words are so powerful that Jesus says, "We will be judged by our words." Our words are powerful enough that God is going to take our words that we say and judge us by them.

Here in Matthew 12:36 Jesus says, "But I say unto you, that idle word that men shall speak, they shall give account thereof, in the Day of Judgment. For by your words you shall be justified, and by your words you shall be condemned."

This shows how important words are, they will either reward you or they will damn you.

In the second chapter of Mark again we see the power of the Word. Where many were gathered together, so many that all could not get inside and Jesus preached the Word to them. And they brought in the sick and with the palsy was lowered down through the roof and Jesus saw their faith and he said unto the sick, "Son your sins be forgiven You."

Again those about Him complained. And Jesus said, "Whether is it easier to say to the sick or the palsy, Your sins are forgiven you, or to say, arise take up your bed and walk?" And Jesus said to the man with the palsy: "Arise and take up your bed and go your way into your house." And he arose and took up his bed and went forth before them all. And they were all amazed and glorified God, saying, "We never saw it on this fashion."

Again it was the word, the Word that Jesus spoke that healed the man. This is what all true ministers of the gospel should preach, the Word of God, the Word of Jesus. When we substitute other things, we are untrue to God, untrue to his fellow man, and untrue to his calling.

Then in John 8:31: "Then Jesus said to the Jews which believed on Him, 'If you continue in My Word, then are you My disciples indeed, and you shall know the truth, and the truth shall make you free.'" Oh, the Power of the spoken Word, the Word of God.

Too many times we leave out the Word, the promises of God, the promises of Jesus, and the Promises of His Word. There are 1722 if's in the Bible, and every one is important, for each tells you what you must do to receive from God's Word. There are conditions to be met if new believers were to remain as true disciples.

In the Bible it reads, if you continue in My Word, the condition to be met with the new believers were to remain as true disciples and have freedom from sin. They were to continue in Jesus' Word, and any man that comes in sin is a servant of sin, but if he keeps the Word, he is a servant of the Lord, the servant of God.

In John 15 we read, "I am the true vine, and the Father is the husband man. Every branch in Me that bears not fruit, he takes away. And every branch that bears fruit, He purges it, that it may bring forth more fruit." Now you are clean through the Word which I have spoken unto you. Immediately (now), He says you are clean when I purge you. Before the cross, before Pentecost, "now" Jesus says. How were they cleansed? They were cleansed by the Word of Jesus, by the power of the Word. Through the Word of God through Jesus Christ made them clean and it is through the Word of Jesus Christ.

What God has given to mankind through His inspiration, the Word of God as He inspired man to tell His Word. This is what makes you clean. The power of the spoken Word.

In Hebrews 4:12: We read, "The Word of God is quick and powerful, and sharper than any two edged sword." There is power, my friends, in the Word of God.

In James 1:22 he states, "Be you doers of the Word and not hearers only, deceiving your own selves." When He says doers, he is saying be performers of the Word. Put the Word into action. Do not be hearers only and deceive yourselves by reasoning. Test your obedience of His word.

James also says in the 19th verse, "My beloved brethren be swift to hear, slow to speak, slow to wrath; for the wrath of man works not the righteousness of God." Receive with meekness the engrafted word, which is able to save your souls. It is by the Word of truth, by the Word of the Bible, which is called seed, when it is implanted into the soul it geminates and springs forth into eternal life. There is power in the Word.

GRANDPA'S LESSONS ABOUT JESUS

What he is saying here is that we, the beloved brethren of Jesus, the adopted sons of God, we should lay apart all of our filthiness in tongue and in word and spread the Word that is inborn, that is inborn in our hearts, through Jesus Christ our Lord and Savior, and through our Father.

What I really want to show you today is that the Power of God which I have just tried to show you through His Word, the Spoken Word, and the Power of God's Word spoken by His Son Jesus. How His spoken Word, not only has the Power to heal, mind body and soul, but it has the power to touch our lives, forgive our sins, to give us salvation, to prepare us for the kingdom of God, and save our souls that we might spent eternity with Him.

So God is telling us to be very careful. Be very careful how we use not only His Words, but also the words that come from our mouth, our brain, from our mind, from our spirit. You know your spirit can speak bad words as well as good words. For there are evil spirits and there is the spirit of God.

You know your life goes the way your tongue is pointed.

Solomon said, in Chapter 17, "He that has knowledge spares his words; and a man of understanding is of an excellent spirit. Even a fool, when he holds his peace, is counted wise; and he that shuts his lips is esteemed a man of understanding."

Even a fool is considered by man to be a wise one if he knows when to speak, and even a wise man is considered a fool if he does not know when to hold his tongue.

GRANDPA'S LESSONS ABOUT JESUS

God says, "He who gossips is a fool should we resist listening to them?" If we hear their words can't we give them our words? Give them God's Words. There is power in God's Word. The words that God puts in our mind and in our spirits have power. God's Word has power. We are the son's of God. We have inherited God's Word through inspiration of God's Word through man, and also directly from God's Spirit to our spirit. Should we run people down? Should we gossip about our fellowmen? Even if what we hear is true, should we go forth and tell others what we heard? Should we go to them and talk direct to them, if we feel a need to discuss the words we hear?

Nowadays many people are being labeled unjustly and very carelessly, and some people are doing it just to be mean because of hate, even in our schools we have youths come forth and tell untrue tales of teachers just to be funny.

What I am trying to tell you today, what I want to tell you is your words have power. Be careful. Choose your words wisely. Think before you speak. Love, build up. Don't destroy. You can never save one who is lost if you destroy them first. Jesus said, "Love them first, Love your enemies." Jesus did not say to love what they do, but He said Love your enemies; because they are My creation. I created them by My Word. And I love them by My Word, it doesn't mean that I am going to accept them into My kingdom if they do not repent. If they do not make a choice and choose Me instead Evil or if between Heaven and Hell. If they do not walk beside Me. I want to give them the opportunity to choose Me and My way, but if they choose not to, they still had the chance.

I want to call your attention to your speech. I want you to call yourself to your attention, to what you say. Yes, even in the house between husband and wife. Even choose what you say, at mealtime with your family, and even what you say with your next-door neighbor.

Choose your words, my friends. You condemn someone and they can be condemned for life. You can ruin them. You can ruin them even if it is true. Don't talk to your neighbor about it. Don't talk to your husband or wife about it. Don't talk to your children about it. If you want to talk about it, talk to God.

Jesus says in Matthew 5:23, "It is so much easier if you go to the problem with or to the person who has the problem." Maybe, you can help him with it. It is better to go over to him in private than to go and make it public.

Let us choose our words. Let us not talk about others unless it is good. The words we choose let them come from the spirit, that God has given us, and not something from our own mind. Let us be careful what we say and how we say it. There will be times, when we hurt someone and didn't mean to, but let us not be to proud to apologize. What we do, let us do in the Name of Jesus Christ our Lord. What we say let us say it in the Name of Jesus. How we live, let it be like Jesus wants us to live. And how we feel about our fellow men, let us have the love that you want Jesus to have for you. The same love that Jesus does have for you. Amen?

We go out into the world and we get dirty. We get tempted; there are a lot of temptations out there. We get sinful desires, and we could go on and on. But the Word of God has a cleansing power. We must wash in the water of the Word daily.

Do you hear me? We must wash with the water of the Word daily. We must cleanse ourselves. And the only way we can cleanse ourselves is with the Word of God.

There is power in the Word of God. There is power in your word.

In 2 Kings 5:2, there was a little Jewish maiden of Syrian captain. She told Naaman about her God and about Elisha. Because of the little girl's word, Naaman went to see Elisha. Naaman had leprosy. Elsha said go and wash in the Jordan seven times, and the flesh shall come clean. Naaman said no, I am too proud to get in the dirty water. His servant said if the prophet had asked you to do some great thing would you have done it? Then went Naaman down and dipped himself seven times. He came out with the flesh of a little child.

The water didn't cleanse him my friend. It was the cleansing by the Word of God. It was the power in the word of God that made him clean. It was the hearing, the obeying of God's Word. Then Naaman said, "Behold now I know, there is no God in all the earth, but in Israel."

It was the Power in the Word.

I want you to know that it is the spoken Word that made the world and all that is in it, even you, it was Jesus spoken Word, that said, "Father, forgive them, for they know not what they do." It was Jesus spoken Word that said, "I go to prepare a place for you that where I am you may be also."

Now go and show others the "Power of the spoken Word."

God Forgives and Forgets

Isaiah 43:25--------"and will not remember my sins."

Jeremiah 31:34----"I will remember their sin no more."

Hebrews 8:12-----"Their sins and their iniquities will I remember
no more."

One of the clearest teachings in the entire Bible is that our God,
the God of the Bible, is omniscient. By that we simply mean that
He see everything, hears everything, therefore He knows
everything.

Let me illustrate:
Friends, our God is never surprised, never shocked. You have
heard people say, "That's news to me." Nothing is news to Him.
He is well aware of everything that is happening on this earth.

Our God is all knowing when it comes to wars. He was not
shocked by the Civil war, World War I, World War II, Korea

war, or the Vietnam War.

That One who said, "There shall be wars and rumors of wars," heard the clanging of the sword, the pop of the musket, and the roar of the cannons in eternity past. All the blood spilt on the battlefields of the world did not come as a surprise to Him who saw Nathanael under the fig tree.

Again I say, "He is not surprised by the rise of wicked Rulers across this world." Hitler was not a rude awakening to our Heavenly Father. Stalin, Mao Tse Tung, and all other tyrants down through the pages of History were nothing more than puppets in the Hand of that One Who "knows our future."

Again He is never "taken aback" by catastrophic events that shake planet earth. He knew the course of the Korean Jetliner destroyed by the murderous Russians. He saw before hand the sinking of the "unsinkable" Titanic. The Chicago fire, and the earthquake that shook San Francisco were not astonishments to Him.

I am simply saying to you that our God is from everlasting to everlasting, all-knowing. The Bible verifies this in verse after verse. Hebrews chapter 4 and verse 13 says, "All the eyes of Him with whom we have to do." My friends, have you forgotten that there are two invisible eyes that run to and fro throughout the whole earth, beholding both the evil and the good?

Again the Bible says in Proverbs 5:21… "For the ways of man are before the eyes of the Lord…" Did you get that Phrase, "the ways of man?" No trip to the grocery store, no visit to the restaurant, no appointment with the dentist escapes His eyes. He knows what goes on behind the closed doors of our homes. He sees the filth, the perverted that taints the streets of our nation. He is sensitive to every decision made in the White House and in your house. Nothing that appears in our newspapers is news to Him.

We read in Jeremiah 23:24, "Can any hide himself in secret places that I shall not see him? Saith the Lord. Do not I fill Heaven and earth? Saith the Lord." The Bible is saying there is not a place too dark, not a spot too remote for a man to hide from the all-knowing God Almighty.

The Psalmist sums it up for us in a beautiful way in Psalm 139: "Whither shall I go from Your Spirit? Or which way shall I flee from Your presence? If I ascend up into Heaven, You art there: If I make my bed in Hell, behold, You are there. If I take the winds of the morning and dwell in the uttermost parts of the sea: even there shall Your hand lead me, and Your right hand shall hold me"... (verses 7-10)

If I could choose one person in the Bible that could put omniscience into our language, I think I would choose Hagar. As she ran from the wrath of Sarah, alone in the wilderness, in deep desperation she cried, "Thou God seest me." (Gen 16:13)

And I believe everyone of us this morning, if we know our Bibles, and full well realize the Power of God, would have to admit, "Thou God seest me." He sees our heart, thoughts, motives, sentiments, and goals. He knows us from the top of our heads to the bottom of our feet. God almighty knows. He is omniscient and may the spirit of God write this upon hearts today.

But wait, in spite of His omniscience, in spite of His all-knowingness, in spite of the fact that He is always there, I say to you, there are at least four instances where God says, "I will remember no more." "I will remember no more." God is actually saying it is possible for him to "forget."

Now it is mighty hard for me to associate forgetfulness with omniscience. Can one who is all knowing and always there experience forgetfulness with finite men like you and me? It's an infirmity of the old flesh. All of us have problems with forgetfulness. We forget names. We forget promises we make. Oh, Yes, Not too long ago someone made a promise to me and I waited and I waited, and I waited and they never did keep the promise. They forgot. We forget promises.

We forget those we love. We forget that birthday card. We forget that anniversary present. We even forget Mom's kiss when we leave the home. We forget the letter to Mom or Dad.

And sad, sad the bitter wail---we even forget almighty God…Psalms 9:17 says, "The wicked shall be turned into hell, and all the nations that forget God." Ecclesiastes 12:1, "Remember now your Creator in the days of your Youth."

Why does God have to remind us to remember Him? Because in this frail flesh, we are prone to forget. Psalm 103:2 says, "Bless the Lord, O my soul, and forget not all His benefits." God has to remind us, the forgetful souls we are, to remember Him.

In First Corinthians 11:24 it says, "This do in remembrance of Me." Speaking of the Lord's Supper. Why did God institute the Lord's Supper? One big reason is so He could give us something that would keep us from forgetting Him. Man is so prone to forget.

But how do we associate forgetfulness, nor remembrance, with omniscience? God says He knows everything. God says He sees everything. God says He hears everything. The Bible verifies that He is omniscient. Yet four times it says, "I will remember no more." How do we explain it?

I think it is easy and both beautiful and precious to the Christian. The omniscient God's forgetfulness is deliberate, part of His grace and mercy.

My friend, the day God saved you He gave you a home in Heaven and indwelled you by His Holy Spirit, and He also forgot your sins, past, present, and future. He put you in a position where you He justified, just as though you had never sinned. Oh! What a blessed thought that is. If we are saved, God has not only forgiven our sins and washed them in His own blood, but he has literally in His mind, forgotten those sins. That moves me, stirs me up, when I think it was my dirty sin that marred his creation that put thorns on the rose bush. And yes, it was my sin that drove Jesus Christ up Calvary's Mountain. It was my shame that brought the prick of the nails in His hands and feet, the thorns in the brow, the spear in His side. I'm overwhelmed to think that God loves me enough not only to forgive my sins; but also to never hold them against me again. Oh! What Grace that is.

I thank God not only for His forgiveness, but also for His divine forgetfulness.

GRANDPA'S LESSONS ABOUT JESUS

For years I was in sin and one of my greatest blessings was to study what happened to my sin when I got saved.

First, God put my sins behind His back; and He said to himself, "That is not enough." Then second, He cast those sins in the depths of the sea, He said that is still not enough. Then He took those sins, removed them as far as the east is from the west, and said, "That is still not enough. They might be found. I will have to do something else." Then He blotted them out, erased them from His memory. He doesn't even remember them.

I like what Charles Spurgeon said about his sins:

> "When I received Christ, neither time with its lapses nor suffering with its fretting, nor doubt with its venom nor death with its terrors can ever resurrect my sins. They are clean gone, clean gone, clean gone from the memory of God."

If that doesn't bless you, my friends, nothing will.

If the devil comes to Jesus Christ tomorrow and he says, "Hey, what about Ed Brock?" Jesus will say, "What about Ed?" And the devil will say. "What about all his sins?" Jesus will look down from His intercessory throne and say, "Oh, I don't recall those." Praise the Lord. Praise the Lord.

Now let us talk about the forgetfulness of God. What does it take for God to forget your sins? What does it require for Him to remove them and blot them out? What is the process of God's forgetfulness?

GRANDPA'S LESSONS ABOUT JESUS

I think there are three things that we need to see. If you need comfort this morning, you'll get some. If you need conviction this morning you'll get some. I believe this message has something in it for every person here today.

When God forgets our sins, He works a miracle upon Himself. Our God is a miracle worker. He can stand on the edge of eternity and with fiery fingertips make worlds. He can stand on the brink of the Red Sea and say, "Come on waters roll back," and there will be a dry path through the sea.

He can stand at Daniel's lion's den and give the beast lockjaw. He can make the sun stand still in its strength. He can open blind eyes. He can unclog deaf ears, and this Miracle Worker can mend hearts.

I want you to see this. When God saved you and me He had to work a miracle on Himself. Let me explain.

In the strictest sense of the word, when we use the word omniscience, that word does not allow for forgetfulness. In the strictest sense of the word, when one is referred to as omniscient (and God is the only one who is), that means He must know everything instantaneously. Everything past, everything present, everything future must be in His mind at every moment. To Him the life of Abraham who lived thousands of years earlier than Peter is just as familiar as Peter's. Omniscience sees all things at one time.

Think about it. In order for God to forget your sins, He had to work a miracle in His own omniscience. He had to erase His mind.

GRANDPA'S LESSONS ABOUT JESUS

Let this speak to your hearts today. God never forgets His universe. He has millions of solar systems to care for. His stars are numberless. He calls them all by name. He tends to the sun and He keeps the planets in their orbits. He doesn't forget His universe, yet He takes time to forget our ugly sins. He blots them out of His mind.

God never forgets His children. I think of the universal flood. The Bible says, "God remembered Noah." See old Jonah in the whale's belly? God didn't forget him. God remembered Jonah. See Elijah by the brook Cherith this morning. How sad he must have been, but the Bible says God didn't forget him. He sent ravens twice a day to feed him. And the one who clothes the lily, that one who makes notice of every sparrow that falls hasn't for gotten and He will not forget you.

You may feel lonely this morning. You may feel like you have gone the last mile of the way. You may feel like the world has passed you by. No, No. God hasn't forgotten you. He never forgets His children.

Oh, isn't it wonderful that the One who cannot forget anything about His children or universe made it so He could forget our sins?

God never forgets kind deeds that are done. He never forgets the cold water given in His name. He never forgets tender words, generous prayers, and useful gifts. He never forgets those tired hours of visitation. He never forgets any good things we do. But the one who cannot forget worked a miracle on His mind so that He would forget our sins the moment He forgave them. God's forgiveness and God's forgetfulness go hand in hand.

I will remember their sin no more.

My friends, God never forgets to smile at us. Never, but I'll tell you what he did do. The mind that cannot forget, the omniscient one who always remembers made it so He would never remember our sins. Hallelujah. If God had not forgotten our sins, if He remembered those sins against us, there would be some things He couldn't do for us.

What are those?
    A.) He could not have adopted us into His Family.
    B.) He could not have let the Holy Spirit come live in us.

The Bible says in Romans 8:16,17: "The Spirit itself bears witness with our spirit that we are the children of God; and if children, then joint heirs with Christ. If so be that we suffer with Him, that we may be also glorified together."

Our bodies are the tabernacle or temple of the Holy Spirit. Do you think that God the Holy Spirit (and He is God) would enjoy living in your body, remembering all the filth of your past? No. He had to make it so that there would be no sin to remember, past, present or future.

    A.) If God remembered our sins He could not be our
        Intercessor. He would be our accuser.
    B.) He could not use us in His service.

There would be no usefulness in any of us if God remembered and held our sins against us. You couldn't teach that Sunday

School Class or drive that bus or preach the Word of God or sing. You couldn't do anything for the Savior if you knew God was still holding your sins against you. You would live in constant grief and guilt and fear. Aren't you glad He removed them?

He worked a miracle upon the records in Heaven.

In Heaven today or at least at one time a record of your sins, and those sins were or are against you. I don't have to go very far to prove that. The Bible says in Romans 14:12, "So then every one of us shall give account of himself to God." How can men give an account if there are not records that make them accountable?

In Daniel 7:10, Daniel looked up and the Bible says, "The Books were opened." He was talking about the divine accounts that are held against the sinner. Note the books are plural. These books are deeds.

If you are here this morning without Jesus Christ, you have an account that must be settled. And the only One who has perfectly settled that in the history of mankind was Jesus Christ when He went to the cross.

He paid the debt for every sin on your record. And the only thing necessary to erase that record is to come to Him and cry. "O God, be merciful to me a sinner." And the whole account will be settled, if you are sincere.

The instant you ask Jesus Christ to save you, God is going to work a miracle on the books.

GRANDPA'S LESSONS ABOUT JESUS

In Isaiah 44:22 it reads, "I have blotted out, as a thick cloud, thy transgressions." The minute you get saved He is going to erase the Books, and He is going to erase His mind; and it will be just as though you have never sinned. All your sins, past, present, and future will have been literally obliterated by the blood of Jesus Christ, and you will be justified forever.

God in His grace remembers our sin no more. When He forgives, He forgets your sins. He wipes the slate clean. He forgets you ever sinned.

He takes off your old Robe and puts you on a new one, a new one that is His righteousness.

Praise God that when He forgives, He forgets. "That is Grace."

What a blessed promise in Isaiah 43:25, "I, EVEN I, AM He that blots out your transgressions for mine own sake, and will not remember your sins."

If there were no Heaven and no Hell, and I knew it, I would still want to be a Christian just to have my sins blotted out and know that God will remember them no more.

No matter how awful your sins may have been, God forgives and forgets. He forgets the horrible sins that you hope no one will ever find out about you, but He also forgets the little sins that perhaps we did not even recognize as sin. Our sins, not in part, but the whole were nailed to the cross, and we bear them no more. Praise the Lord, it is well with our souls.

I can assure you if you have come to the foot of the cross and sincerely repented, your sins have been forgiven and forgotten. You have God's Word on it.

Edward E. Brock, Jr. is a native Hoosier who served in the Army Air Corp during World War II, worked for the Pennsylvania Railroad, Penn Central, and Conrail for 43 years, is a respected Indiana country pastor, as well as a great-grandfather, grandfather, father, and husband of Blanche for almost 70 years.